"Homosexuality is more than a biblical debate about who's right and who's wrong. Everything converges in the pastoral and the personal context, and Andrew Marin—unlike any writer I've seen—deals with real humans in real human contexts. We desperately need this book; it has the potential to shift the evangelical movement in a more compassionate direction."

SCOT MCKNIGHT, Karl A. Olsson Professor in Religious Studies, North Park University

"The evangelical church, with a few exceptions, has been stuck with three options when it comes to our thinking and action concerning the gay community. Some remain silent because they're fearful and aren't sure what they believe. Others engage in loud and acerbic speech-making, convinced that they must first address 'conclusive' biblical truth on this special sin before any possible conversation could even begin. Still others attempt to adopt a 'love the sinner but hate the sin' perspective that sounds good on paper but seems to play out in reality as distancing from those perceived sinners. Andrew Marin, thankfully, breaks through these three options with the 'Why haven't we been doing this all along?' approach of love and dialogue. Reading this book feels like Marin just called a time-out, and asked us all to sit in a circle and talk turkey."

MARK OESTREICHER, president, Youth Specialties

"One of the most important conversations happening in the church. And one of the most divisive. Andrew Marin is a fresh, gracious, innovative voice in the dialogue. For Marin, this is not about a hot-button 'issue'—it is about a face, a friend, a child of God. It is about Jesus, whose love many find hard to grasp because of what they have felt from his followers. Andrew reminds us that, whether conservative or liberal, we can have great ideas and still be mean and self-righteous. And ultimately they will know we are Christians, not by our proof-texting, but by our love."

SHANE CLAIBORNE, author, activist, recovering sinner

Andrew Marin

Foreword by Brian McLaren

Love Is an Orientation

Elevating the Conversation

with the Gay Community

IVP Books
An imprint of InterVarsity Press
Downers Grove, Illinois

InterVarsity Press
P.O. Box 1400, Downers Grove, IL 60515-1426
World Wide Web: www.ivpress.com
Email: email@ivpress.com

InterVarsity Press® is the book-publishing division of InterVarsity Christian Fellowship/ USA®, a student movement active on campus at hundreds of universities, colleges and schools of nursing in the United States of America, and a member movement of the International Fellowship of Evangelical Students. For information about local and regional activities, write Public Relations Dept., InterVarsity Christian Fellowship/USA, 6400 Schroeder Rd., P.O. Box 7895, Madison, WI 53707-7895, or visit the IVCF website at <www.intervarsity.org>.

Design: Cindy Kiple

Images: grunge paper: Duncan Walker/iStockphoto
three males walking: Nicki Pardo/Getty Images

ISBN 978-0-8308-3626-0

Printed in the United States of America ∞

Library of Congress Cataloging-in-Publication Data

Marin, Andrew P.
Love is an orientation: elevating the conversation with the gay
community / Andrew P. Marin.
p. cm.
Includes bibliographical references.
ISBN 978-0-8308-3626-0 (pbk.: alk. paper)
1. Homosexuality—Religious aspects—Christianity. 2. Sex
role—Religious aspects—Christianity. 3. Love—Religious
aspects—Christianity. I. Title.
BR115.H6M355 2009
261.8'35766—dc22

                                                                2008054477

P 19 18 17 16 15 14 13 12 11 10 9 8 7 6 5 4 3 2

Y 24 23 22 21 20 19 18 17 16 15 14 13 12 11 10 09

Dedicated to Barry—

Only you can grasp what you have meant to my life

Contents

Foreword

Fools rush in where angels fear to tread, the old saying goes. But the same is true for heroes. Heroes rush into burning buildings to save complete strangers. Heroes rush to places of famine and war and epidemic to bring food and shelter and medicine. Heroes rush into brewing conflicts to take the risk of making peace. They aren't fools: they know about the danger, disease, crossfire and conflict that will surround them. But they have the courage to throw themselves in anyway, risking their own safety for the common good.

Today we are blessed with some spiritual heroes who also refuse to keep their distance and protect themselves until engagement becomes less risky, or maybe even respectable. Fully aware of the risks, they rush in—to groups that are aflame with hot and spreading conflict, to enclaves of wounded people who have been excluded and rejected, to communities torn by contention and dissension. These heroes seek to be agents of healing, understanding, reconciliation and peace. They don't worry about the criticism they will receive. (Well, they may worry, but they don't let it stop them.) They know they'll be misunderstood and vilified. They know that some of the meanest people on earth are sincere, well-intentioned religious people who believe in their religion so fervently they would die for it but also would kill for it—literally or metaphorically. Yet these heroes still step forward, not shrinking back, driven by a force that is greater than self-preservation.

In so doing, they are following the same Leader, Jesus Christ, who did not seek his own interests, but those of others. He knew what it would mean to give himself—to live and die not just for others but for *sinners*—yet he endured the cross, counted its shame as nothing, all for the joy set before him: the joy of reconciling humanity with itself and with God. I have had the great honor to know many of these kinds of heroes in my life. Most of them have been older than me, but it's a great joy now to meet more and more who are younger. One of them is Andrew Marin. You're about to read his first book. I'd like to introduce it through this parable.

▪ ▪ ▪

I don't want to be closed-minded or judgmental, but in good conscience I simply can't approve of the lifestyle. I personally believe it's a choice, not something predestined or forced upon anyone by anyone. I understand that parental upbringing is undoubtedly a big factor and that some people believe genes play a role in predisposing people to this orientation, but I also know that adults are responsible for their behavior, and the behaviors associated with this lifestyle are no exception.

On the one hand, I believe that we live in a free country, and people should be free to do what they think is right. But on the other hand, I believe freedom has limits—one limit being where others are hurt by the chosen lifestyle. And this lifestyle, there can be no mistake, is hurting a lot of people. Families are being torn apart by it, and churches and denominations too.

Everybody has an opinion on this controversial lifestyle, but I believe God's opinion is the one that matters most, and there is absolutely no question what God's opinion is according to the Bible. This orientation and the behaviors associated with it are thoroughly condemned, especially by Jesus. He was very compassionate toward many groups of people, but there is one group he had an absolute and uncompromising commitment to confront and expose, and it was those who dishonor themselves and others as humans made in the image of God by engaging in this lifestyle and its practices.

When people choose this lifestyle, they often cut themselves off from everyone who doesn't agree with them. They end up being assimilated and absorbed into closed communities where only their own voices and views are heard, and everyone who disagrees is mocked and condemned, often with very strong language. They often see their community as superior and become incapable of speaking respectfully to or of those of us who cannot in good conscience agree with them. Some of them go so far as to claim that God made them the way they are, pushing onto God the responsibility for their own choices and behaviors.

Some, after giving themselves over completely to the lifestyle, have a crisis of conscience. But when they want to leave, their leaders and peers depict their changing perspective as a betrayal and pressure them to stay, often using fear tactics to intimidate them and keep them in their community. Special ministries have formed to help people exit the lifestyle, recover from the abuse and pain the community has been known to impose, and be reoriented to a healthier life and perspective. But even with professional therapy, many people feel they have been wounded for life by what they've experienced, and many, looking back on their years "inside," compare the lifestyle to an addiction.

Spokespeople for the lifestyle can seem very educated and scholarly. They claim that their position has a long history behind it. They often quote scientific studies and back up their assertions with emotional anecdotes. Sometimes they seek to gain sympathy by claiming they are being mistreated and persecuted for being outspoken about their views. But they tend to ignore other strands of history and scientific research that contradict their position, and they ignore anecdotes that don't fit with their predetermined conclusions, and they minimize the persecution they inflict on others.

Advocates are eager to recruit others into their "love" as they call it. Many organizations raise huge sums of money to recruit youth and children into their chosen way of life, and they have been extremely adept at using media—radio, TV and now the Internet—to gain an aura of credibility and legitimacy. They organize huge events and mass rallies to celebrate their growing clout and demonstrate that they are proud of who they are and what they stand for. Everyone knows how much influence they have in our political system, and how one political party in particular panders for their votes. But look at the countries where this lifestyle runs rampant, and you'll get an idea what our nation will be like if some of us don't have the courage to stand up and speak up. Wherever this lifestyle spreads, a whole host of social problems inevitably follows.

Yes, activists may use the word *love* to justify their behavior, but those who disagree with them are seldom treated with love. Many of us have already faced the scorn of the activists who promote this chosen lifestyle and defend it as legitimate and even godly. For doing so we have received hate mail peppered with a wide range of threats and abusive speech, with many calling for our damnation. But even so, we have learned that we must not respond to hate with hate; we must love these people and seek to help them, even though we do not approve of their behavior.

■ ■ ■

You've probably realized by now that this parable isn't talking about "the gay lifestyle" but rather "the judgmental lifestyle," the kind of "take-the-splinter-out-of-your-brother's-eye" religiosity that Jesus talked about in the Sermon on the Mount. (If you didn't realize it, try going back and rereading it in that light.) As someone born and raised in a strict, conservative church—actually, the term *fundamentalist* would have fit us perfectly—I've seen a good bit of judging and condemning and dividing and excluding in my lifetime, and I know how good and holy and utterly righteous it can feel to indulge in. Having served as a pastor most of my adult life, I've seen the judgmental lifestyle at work in quite a few parishioners too, and I was more than once on the receiving end of their attempts at splinter removal. But more personally, I must admit I've practiced more

than my share of the judging lifestyle too—although I have generally been careful to call it "discerning" when I've been the one doing
it. I guess I could say, with songwriter Joni Mitchell, that I've known
judgment "from both sides now."

And that's one reason Andrew Marin's book seems to me to be so
important, and why I'm so glad this emerging leader has been given
the courage to write it. As you've probably heard (note *UnChristian*),
among young adults in the United States, the terms *evangelical* and
born again are now most strongly associated with the characteristics
of being anti-gay and judgmental. Whatever your opinion on same-
sex orientation, you have to admit that Jesus didn't say, "They'll know
you are my disciples by your firm stance on divisive social issues."
No, he said we'll be known as his disciples for another reason . . . and
that's what Andrew is pursuing in these pages.

When you come to the last page, Andrew won't ask you to agree
with his opinions about the gay orientation or lifestyle. In fact, he
won't indulge in a lot of opinion polemics. Instead he will try to help
you understand what he has learned by listening with an open and
compassionate heart to gay women and men. And he will try to help
you respond to gay people in your world in a more mature and compassionate way too. And in the end, he'll ask you to agree with him
on one main thing: that the orientation and lifestyle of love is the
right and only way for true followers of Jesus.

He'll do so because he has surrendered himself wholeheartedly
to that orientation of love. It's not just superficial tolerance he's after, and it's not just the ever-popular "love in word only" that uses
the word but doesn't suffer the consequences. No, the love to which
Andrew has surrendered himself is the amazing, unfathomable,
give-your-all love of God. That love could never be captured in a
word or even in ten thousand words. Ultimately, it was best shown
in a life, and in a death, and in a resurrection.

This love reaches out to all of us—those who experience rejection
and those who reject, those who react and those who are reacted
against, those who are stereotyped and those who stereotype, those

who fear and those who are feared. It isn't elicited by the loveability of its object, but rather it flows from the all-generous and holy, holy, holy orientation of its Subject, God. And it is into this generous, holy orientation that we are about to be invited in a new and deep way, in the nitty-gritty of one of today's most vexing and contentious subjects. May the Spirit of the living, loving God use the words of this courageous young writer to draw us deeper into the orientation and lifestyle of divine love. May we, each in our own way, become heroes in the cause of love.

Brian McLaren
Christmas, 2008

P.S. I'd like to ask you to do Andrew a favor, OK? When you turn the last page, some of you will be disappointed that Andrew didn't go further. And others of you will be concerned that Andrew went too far. Between here and the last page, you'll have your checklists in mind, waiting to see if he says and doesn't say the things you want him to. If Andrew simply fulfilled your script, or someone else's, this book would hardly be worth reading; it would just say things that have been said before. So why not let Andrew share what's uniquely on his heart? Why not listen, and appreciate, and learn?

Introduction

When My Friends Came Out

It's Tuesday evening at 7 p.m. As I have done each Tuesday evening for the past year, I am sitting in the first booth next to the front door at my favorite diner, talking with a man whom I love as a brother. The diner is in a storefront located in the heart of a rainbow-flagged, sex-shop-filled, bar- and club-laced, gay-inhabited ten-block neighborhood on Chicago's North Side known as Boystown.

Sitting across from me is a forty-six-year-old Orthodox Jewish man with AIDS on a unique life-ending quest: to figure out who *Yeshua* is and discover what God's original plan was for his life before it got derailed with this horrible disease.

My friend became infected with HIV almost thirty years ago, and all his friends who acquired HIV at the same time are now dead. He has been alone for a long time, one last survivor from what many originally thought of as God's final judgment on the gay community.

In the hospital a few years earlier he was lying in his own death-bed—sunken eyes and cheeks, jaundiced skin and a weight of one hundred pounds—waiting to meet the same fate as everyone he once knew. His family flew in from the East Coast and Israel to say goodbye to their shamed grandson, son, brother, uncle and cousin. The hours passed, the goodbyes were spoken, and the wait for death began.

In what his doctors called a miracle, my friend was healed. Life came back to his eyes, color came back to his skin, and his weight rapidly increased. Could it have been the cocktailed pills that healed him? Was it the IV that pumped potent medication into his blood twenty-four hours a day that pushed him back to life? Or was it rather a wake-up call that God had something more in store for him?

So here we are, every Tuesday night, meeting to intentionally seek our Father's face as we journey to discover why this man's fate is life and not an early death.

This is the neighborhood I live in and the world I have been called to. These are the stories that have become my everyday life.

BEGINNINGS

I am a straight, white, conservative, Bible-believing, evangelical male. I was raised in a Christian home in a conservative suburb of Chicago and grew up in a large evangelical church. And I wanted absolutely nothing to do with the gay, lesbian, bisexual and transgender (GLBT) community.

Looking back on my upbringing, I don't remember hearing anything explicitly defaming the GLBT community from either my church or my parents. Homosexuality just grossed me out, and I sure wasn't about to have an in-depth conversation with my pastor or my parents about the subject. I just knew that my beliefs were right. I saw gay people on TV. I saw pictures of cross-dressers in newspapers and magazines. For the first nineteen years of my life I was the biggest Bible-banging homophobic person I knew. I used derogatory language about gay people without ever thinking twice about what I believed or said. I didn't care about the gay community nor did I ever want to care about them. "Don't ask, don't tell," "Don't see, don't care," "Out of sight, out of mind": those philosophies all worked great for me—until, that is, the summer after my freshman year in college.

That June one of my best friends, who went to the same university I did, told me that she needed to talk. It sounded serious but I didn't think anything about it; best friends have deep conversations all the time. She invited me over to her apartment for dinner. As I sat on her beat-up futon in the living room I kept hearing her drop things in the kitchen. This was not at all like her, and I asked repeatedly what was bothering her. She finally came into the living room, sat right next to me, gave me one of her big hugs that I loved so much, snapped her head directly in line with mine and abruptly told me, "Don't tell anyone, but I'm a lesbian."

OUT

Is she serious?! I tried to pull myself together and look cool, like I had known all along, but I knew I was breathing heavy—I was totally flustered. The horror, pain and dumb-foundedness I felt shook me. She didn't look like a lesbian . . . I knew she had boyfriends . . . I'd even met them! What is going on? I looked her dead in the eyes and panicked. Is there a right response?

I took a shaky breath and promptly said, "OK then, what's to eat?"

The next morning I woke up feeling strange, almost like there had been a death in my family. But I thought, *If I can pretend long enough that she didn't come out to me, I can actually keep my best friend.*

The next month I received a call from another one of my best friends. She too had something to tell me. It was dusk when I got to her apartment where I was greeted by a barrage of hugs from some of our other friends. That night we all hung out and had a great time. When just about everyone else was asleep she pulled me into her room where her roommate was sleeping. She sat me down, grabbed my arms, looked at me with a warm gaze and, in a whisper faint enough that only I could hear, said, "I'm gay. I'm a lesbian. I've always been this way."

I kept quiet because I didn't want to cause a scene in front of everyone, but inside I kept thinking, *No, no, no. Not her too!* I felt queasy, and questions rapidly exploded in my mind: *How could she be a lesbian? What the heck was I missing? Did my other best friend know about her? Did she know about my other best friend? Were they together? Do I have a stamp on my forehead that says, "Gay? Need a best friend?"*

I just couldn't take it; my stomach churned, my head hurt, and I felt like I was going to throw up. All I could do at that point was lie down and go to sleep.

As the sun rose I woke up, said my goodbyes and drove home in tears. I knew what the Bible says. My friends knew what the Bible says. They knew that I knew that they knew what the Bible says. How could I get past the gigantic pink elephant in the room and keep being friends with these lesbians?

The very next month I was sitting with another good friend in his car the night before he was to return to his university downstate. We had been friends since second grade; we grew up in the same elementary school, middle school and high school. We had gone to the same church, had the same friends and played the same sports. He said he needed to talk to me, and jokingly I said, "Let me guess. Now you're going to tell me you're gay, right?" As soon as I uttered those words he began to cry, nodding his head yes. What more was there to say? Tears started flowing down my face, and we sat in his car and cried together.

Three best friends, three consecutive months. I started to ask God why he would give me three friends in the one community that I had purposefully spoken against all of these years! I spent the next few weeks searching for anything that I could get my hands on that would offer reason to that unreasonable summer. Then it came. I felt the Spirit tell me, "If you want to find the truth, you have to seek it for yourself." I knew exactly what that meant. I called my three best friends and told them we needed to get together.

When we were finally able to talk I could not hold back my emotions and my feelings. In one fell swoop of nervous energy I blurted, "I believe that being gay is a sin. It's a choice. You can change. You're going to hell. You're going to start obsessively drinking and doing drugs. You're going to be promiscuous. You're going to be butch and flamboyant and you're going to get HIV/AIDS or STDs at some point. "Now give me something that explains what I feel! Help me understand!

"Oh yeah, and all three of you are gay."

We talked until the early hours of the morning. Each shared about their lives—what life was like trying to deal with these thoughts and feelings on their own, what it was like to have me as a best friend, how they weren't sure whether they were right or wrong, weird or normal, sinful or not sinful, whether this was nature or nurture, their fault or God's fault. Each of them had their own answers, but we all realized that a journey had just begun.

IMMERSION

People tell me the decision I made at that point was the strangest decision they have ever heard. In order to completely answer the Holy Spirit's call, I decided to fully immerse myself in the GLBT community. My ultimate goal was to become, as I put it back then, "the most involved, gayest straight dude on the face of the earth." I sought out only GLBT friends, went exclusively to GLBT events and functions, and spent my time hanging out at GLBT bars and clubs to talk, learn and listen.

I began this immersion during my sophomore year in college. I would go to Boystown with my best friends upwards of four nights a week. I would go to a GLBT bar or club, order a Pepsi, find a corner to sit in and wait for someone to talk to. Every time I would walk into one of the establishments, heads would turn and the whispers would begin. I'll never forget the very first time I went to a gay club. No more than five minutes after entering, I was approached by someone who asked me if I was gay. When I said no, they smiled, turned around to a waiting group of friends, pointed at me and yelled, "I told you so! Pay up!"

I have since discovered that the GLBT community has an extremely accurate "gaydar." They can pick out a straight guy from ten miles away! The unique side effect to their gaydar was that I became a walking icebreaker by doing nothing other than stepping into a world I knew nothing about. A flow of people would approach me asking why I was there—what I was doing and why I would even care to visit. Nightly, I ended up in life-altering conversations for hours upon hours. After a while I started to notice two very specific trends. One, people would inevitably end up in tears telling me their life story. Two, the tears were usually brought on by a story about a negative experience with Christians or a church. The weird thing was, I never told any of them that I was a Christian.

I started to realize that there was something happening within the GLBT community regarding God, faith and religion. I didn't know what to do with this new information, so I just stored it away and waited for the Lord to move next.

THE BIBLE STUDY

I attended college on a baseball scholarship, and the semester previous to my friends coming out, at the urging of some of my teammates, I had started a Bible study for athletes. One of my lesbian friends eventually asked if she could come. Of course I said yes, but inside I was puzzled as to why a lesbian would want to come to a Bible study. I couldn't understand why people who are gay would be interested in studying a book that condemns their life. But she showed up and really liked it, and ended up telling some of her gay and lesbian friends about it. Those friends started asking me eternally significant questions and then went on to tell their gay and lesbian friends, and the process continued to repeat itself. Soon I was receiving random phone calls from GLBT people all over the city of Chicago and its suburbs—all ages, races and demographic backgrounds. Within six weeks the Bible study went from seven straight baseball players to me and thirty-six GLBT people meeting in smaller groups throughout the week; all the straight people left because they were too weirded out by what was happening.

The totality of the group grew to over one hundred people who were either gay, lesbian, bisexual or transgender, and me. One week two older men pulled me aside and told me that they had left their gay-affirming church and were treating our time together as their church. Humbled and yet confused, I walked in front of everyone and asked two questions: "Why do you come? Why do you tell others to come?"

Their profound answers, along with many new concepts and questions, will be thoroughly unpacked within the following chapters as we move forward and learn how to elevate the conversation in order to build peaceful and productive bridges with gay, lesbian, bisexual and transgender people.

BUILDING BRIDGES

Evangelical churches, families and individuals all across the country are being challenged by the GLBT community. The dichotomized relationship between evangelicals and the GLBT community has a traumatic history and continues to grow further apart. Each group talks past the other rather than to the other group. The result is that, by and large, evangelicals know gay people only in a narrowly focused, two-dimensional light, and the GLBT community is left to search for God without the body of Christ to assist them, encourage them and validate their human existence as children of God.

Some of what you are going to read is not going to be easy to hear or grasp; it will challenge everything you ever thought about the GLBT community. Believers need to hear, understand and fight through their own hesitations and learn about the GLBT community's arguments, theories and stories as valid to their experiences in this world. Their lives are as real as ours, and our faith in Jesus Christ requires us to meticulously seek honest transparency not only within the GLBT community but in ourselves as well.

For much of the last decade I have journeyed to the threshold of everything I thought was true. My organization, The Marin Foundation, has been all over the country working to elevate the conversation between conservative Christians and the GLBT community. Learning how to build bridges with a GLBT family member, friend, coworker, congregant or local GLBT community can be the most difficult task ever brought to your doorstep. This book will challenge how you think about and relate to gays and lesbians. We will explore the principles and techniques that The Marin Foundation has found invaluable, keeping aware of our very real differences but also of the hurdles that unnecessarily complicate our conversations and relationships.

Along the way we'll consider the psychology of sexual identity, the social challenges of being gay in a straight culture, the history of evangelical-GLBT dialogue and the current state of affairs. We'll also look at how the question of homosexuality has shaped different people's reading of Scripture and revisit the question of what, ultimately, the good news of the gospel is. Finally, we'll explore a distinctive set of practical commitments to help these two divergent communities work together toward something supremely important to both: the love of God and the spiritual yearning in our souls.

My experience at The Marin Foundation has also been informed by our unique research project—the largest of its kind—looking into the religious convictions and experiences of the GLBT community throughout the United States. Gay, lesbian, bisexual and transgender people across the country have told us their stories about religion and described their understanding of God; evangelicals will be surprised to learn that when the ambient noise of genetics, psychology and politics is tuned down, the GLBT community is ultimately like every other: compelled by the gospel as they taste and see that the Lord is good.

1

We Don't Need Your God!

Many Christians see a GLBT person's "out and proud" status and automatically group that individual into a broad category of God-hating militants. To begin this journey of building bridges, however, we need to put ourselves, as much as heterosexual Christians can, into the cloudy circumstances and daily life of what it is to live attracted to people of the same sex.

THEY'RE JUST KIDS

Research now reports that the average age of someone who first realizes a same-sex attraction is thirteen years old. It also shows that the average age of someone who declares their sexual orientation as gay, lesbian, bisexual or transgender is fifteen years old! Think back to when you were thirteen, fourteen and fifteen years old and add onto those already insecure, awkward years the extra burden of having these new, sometimes frightful sexual thoughts and not knowing where they came from. Who do you tell—your parents? Church? Friends? Each of whom will more than likely be completely grossed out, totally ashamed or thoroughly disappointed by the news. The risk is just too big, and therefore most kids don't tell anyone.

Sexuality surrounds our youth each day, whether or not Christian adults want to admit this reality. I have had the opportunity to meet with various high school Gay-Straight Alliances (GSA), and each time

I am taken aback by the openness with which these kids talk about their sexual experiences. The first time I had this opportunity, twenty-two young faces hung intently on my words, looking for any reassurance that they were normal. One thing was clear to me that day: if I were a high school kid in that environment and one of the GSA kids asked me what I thought about their sexuality, I wouldn't have known how to respond. I do know this much though: it wouldn't have been pretty. I might only be a decade removed from high school, but I learned really quickly that the pendulum of sexuality has drastically shifted toward a culture of open experimentation.

I was recently conducting a workshop at a church in a Chicago suburb. During the question-and-answer time a woman sitting in the front raised her hand. As I called on her I saw her eyes immediately turn bloodshot red. She quickly reached for the Kleenex that had been hiding in her pocket, and before she could get a word out, she began to cry.

As she tried to pull herself together she shared that a month earlier her fourteen-year-old son came home from school and asked if gay people were going to hell. She thought that was a strange question, and asked why he wanted to know. He told her that two of his best friends, whom she knew very well, had just "come out" to him. At that moment she burst out with praise to God that her son didn't tell her *he* was gay, but she quickly realized by her stoic son's expression that he didn't care for the celebration; he just wanted an answer. He wanted that answer because the very first question his friends asked him after they came out was if he thought they were going to hell. Someone told the friends they were indeed going to hell, and with a tear in his eye the son just wanted some reassurance that it wasn't true.

At this point the mom finally realized the extreme pressure this was causing her son and didn't know what to tell him. As any caring mother would do she broke down herself because her fourteen-year-old son was now confronted with a situation neither she nor her husband knew how to handle. She went on that night to tell me that she did the best she could but nonetheless still felt inadequate, because as parents they never wanted to think in advance how to explain something so difficult. "You try to keep your children from certain things but that can only happen for so long. I failed my son because I was scared to think about it myself."

THE BATTLEFIELD OF COMING OUT

Most adolescents experiencing same-sex attraction are too frightened to say anything to anybody for fear of what might happen, who else might find out and what the potentially negative ramifications might be. So they lock it deep inside and try to somehow deal with it on their own.

John, a thirty-seven-year-old man, is just starting to understand himself and his faith. Twenty-two years earlier, locked in his room one Sunday morning, John finally understood what was making him so different from every other boy his age: he was gay. Day after day, tears flowed down his face—in private. He socially shut himself off from everyone he knew because he was overwhelmed with the thought that someone might suspect something. His constant self-analysis began to consume all of his thoughts, and he continued to grow further away from everything he once loved. His secret trapped him and he didn't see any way out.

John's story is like that of many others when they first realize their same-sex attraction, except that he had Christian parents and Christian brothers and sisters. They loved the Lord with all of their hearts, as did he. John went to a Christian high school and was heavily involved in his church and youth group. He volunteered in his local community and in college attended the largest, most well-known evangelical university in the country, where he was prestigiously elected student body president.

Through all of these outward Christian successes John's soul was scarred because he thought he had to keep his attractions a secret. Daily he wondered why God would let *him* have these problems. He had decided at age fifteen, when the attractions first began, that he would earnestly pray one prayer every night: "Lord, when I wake up in the morning please just let me be straight like everyone else."

John prayed that prayer every night until he was *thirty years old.* And every morning for fifteen years he woke up dejected and broken because he still had the same attractions he never wanted in the first place. By the time I met him he was thirty-four years old, and like many others in his situation had determined that one of two conclusions must be true.

The first possibility is that there is no God because he had not answered the one prayer they ever prayed. A number of people I have known over the years were so initially terrified by the realization of a same-sex attraction that they gave up all other desires. They wanted nothing for their birthdays, Christmas or any holiday other than for God to take these feelings away. I have also known others who have substituted superficial desires—material goods, popularity, etc.—in place of their intimate desires so as to try to cover up all of the pain and shame they felt for being attracted to the same sex.

Too often the intense pressure of getting rid of these gay erotic thoughts from either extreme overtakes people's lives and dominates their existence for so long that it's all they can think about. This perseveration consumes their entire being and, with so much persisting hurt and pain, they wonder why, if there is a God, he would let them suffer so much. There must not be a God after all.

The second possibility people come to is that if there is a God, perhaps he is not answering their one prayer because they are already condemned to hell for their same-sex feelings. If that is true, people such as John believe that they might as well fully immerse themselves in the gay life because it doesn't matter one way or the other.

And what struck me as so significant about these two thoughts was the fact that the man sitting in front of me pouring his tortured heart out was the former student body president of the most well-known evangelical university in the country! At that moment I realized this topic was no longer the "battle of all eternal sanctity" as I had always been told it was. This topic, just like John, is about building bridges to those among us whom we let go without a second thought.

WHAT HAPPENS ON THE OTHER SIDE
OF REALIZATION?

What happens in the long run to a person who prays the same prayer every night and wakes up every morning not having that prayer answered? If John lives to be seventy-five, he could look forward to 21,915 consecutive mornings of wondering whether there really is a God, or convincing himself that he's condemned to hell because of attractions he can't figure out.

The majority of GLBT people whom I have met over my nine years of being immersed in their community—believers and nonbelievers, black and white, men and women—have told me the same thing: when they first realized their same-sex thoughts and attractions they started to pray that God would take those unwanted feelings away. Even atheists have told me that they were willing to put their unbelief in God aside in the hope that he would make them straight like everyone else.

It's tempting from the outside to come up with a clever rebuttal, to justify the pain GLBT people have endured or to explain why the same-sex attractions persist. "They only prayed for . . . They didn't seek outside help . . . They didn't tell anyone . . . They should have done . . ."

Christians need to start willfully planting themselves in the middle of some very uncomfortable places—making a conscious commitment to stay in that place with the GLBT community. In 1963 Martin Luther King Jr. was locked up in a jail in Birmingham, Alabama. In a letter addressed to his fellow clergymen, King reflected on his life's work to that point and said: "I must confess that I am not afraid of the word 'tension.' I have earnestly opposed violent tension, but there is a type of constructive, nonviolent tension which is necessary for growth."

The Christian community has been running from that constructive, nonviolent tension for too long when it comes to gays and lesbians. The productive growth that Martin Luther King Jr. was talking about only comes retrospectively, after much time has been spent immersed in tension-filled areas with what we are most uneasy about. Those tension-filled areas are dirty, disgusting, confusing, overbearing and uncomfortable. And they're worth every minute for the kingdom we so boldly claim ourselves to be a part of. I was brought to one such tension-filled place by a man named Chuck.

Chuck had been attending The Marin Foundation's community classes and programs for about a year. He hadn't said more than two words the entire time, but one night his entire life's history suddenly came crashing to the surface. In the 1950s Chuck had been kicked out of his home in a small farm town because his traditional believing parents didn't know how to handle the admission of his sexuality. Chuck packed up all of his belongings and moved to Chicago. He had nothing to his name other than what he squeezed into his tiny car.

At nineteen years old, living on his own and not knowing anybody, he took out loans, got a few odd jobs, and ended up putting himself through college and grad school. Over the years he searched for a place to fit in because he was never athletic, never liked the bar scene and just wanted to feel loved. After many years Chuck decided to give Christianity a try again. Even though the Christian faith was the basis for his parents' rejection, Chuck always thought there was something unique about believers. He started to attend a church and was scared for anyone to find out he was gay, so he just kept it to himself. After a while he felt safe and confident that he could tell someone he trusted. Unfortunately his worst fears were realized when that person told everyone and he got kicked out of the second place that ever felt like home.

Without any other options, he immersed himself into the large GLBT community in Chicago and began to meet some wonderful friends who were also gay and knew what he was going through. Thirty-five years later Chuck has a well-paying job, a nice house, a nice car, a loving partner and a supportive group of friends who have never turned their back on him.

One night during class I looked at Chuck, about to ask him a question. He started shaking. Seconds later he choked out the burdensome message he had been yearning to say for the last forty years of his life: "Why do I need you, and why do I need your God? I don't need either!"

And then it was over. Raw tears of freedom replaced the tears of entrapment he had been crying for the majority of his life.

At that moment I was simultaneously an innocent bystander and the target of his words. I had no idea what was going through his head or why tonight he decided to free himself of what he'd kept pent up for almost half a century. I stood there soaking in the excruciating emotion that was bleeding out of his pores, realizing that his first experience of emotional freedom in almost fifty years came by telling a Christian he didn't need him or his God.

But what kept running through my head was, why even come to The Marin Foundation in the first place if those were his thoughts? Why keep coming back? Why tell other gay and lesbian people to come as well? What could I possibly be offering him if he didn't need me or my God?

Snapping back to reality from my cloud of questions, I peered around the room and saw the faces of thirteen other gay men and lesbian women. At that moment I realized that Chuck had released what they all felt and yet never had the emotional energy or raw courage to vocalize.

Each day of my life working with the GLBT community I see the tears and I hear the pain. But for the first time that day I *felt* the tears and I *felt* a pain I had never experienced before. In a traditional interpretation of Scripture, gay sexual behavior is defined as sin, and because of that many Christians have taken that sin and, in their mind, rightfully ostracized an entire group of people. Think about what that means to a gay or lesbian person who is trying to discover, or rediscover, church. Even if they were to attend a service or involve themselves in a small group or church activities, they would still be separate, and could never be considered equal unless they became like everyone else—a sinner who doesn't sin with same-sex attraction. Where is the hope in that expectation, when many GLBT people are not being met where they are?

That night Chuck let a conservative, Bible-believing, evangelical, straight male into the real life of someone in the GLBT community. I felt bad; I felt guilty. My soul ached because in some small way I finally began to scrape the surface of the intense depth and despair that the GLBT community feels. Only they could truly understand what they have experienced. And all that I, my Christian church, my Christian friends and anyone else who has never been attracted to someone of the same sex should have been doing was to be there in support and love, doing our best to willfully convene in the middle of Chuck's place of tension—trying to grasp what only he knows he has been through.

When everyone's eyes started to dry, I asked Chuck what brought on that moment. "I come to these classes because it brings me back to the one thing that I always wanted. But I'm too scared to let myself fall for this again. So I just sit and listen and try to feel blessed in this place as I pray that there is somehow a spot for me in heaven."

Since that night I occasionally hear from other gay and lesbian people the phrase *I don't need you and I don't need your God*. My soul breaks each time I hear those words. I realize now, though, that Chuck's words about God were an expression of yearning, not hatred. They were a yearning to reclaim a past that can never be reclaimed. They expressed a yearning to have a different life as he struggles with the knowledge that life can never be done over again. Over the years I have clearly learned, through experiences just like Chuck's, that at a baseline level all the GLBT community wants from God is (a) to have the same intimate relationship with God that evangelicals claim to have; and (b) to safely enter into a journey toward an inner reconciliation of who they are sexually, spiritually and socially. Really, these simple desires are not that different from ours.

PRECONCEIVED IDEAS

I remember sitting on my couch in May 2007 watching CNN's coverage of the death of Jerry Falwell. I was horrified at what a series of prominent GLBT leaders, some of whom I know personally, and everyday GLBT people walking on the street had to say about him only hours after his passing. The poignancy and disgust of their feelings toward this man and the life he lived were clear and concise, and it hit me square between my eyes.

The larger issue CNN's piece brought to light was that if Christians want to lessen the current disconnect we cannot continue to live brandished as a homophobic people. Yet that is exactly what we are doing. It really doesn't matter whether we believe these homophobic perceptions by the GLBT community are fact or fiction. The truth remains that when it comes to gays and lesbians and evangelical Christianity, perception is reality. The majority of the people negatively talking about Jerry Falwell that night had never met him. But there is an undercurrent of preexisting negative perceptions of Christianity's traditional belief system that utterly repulses gays and lesbians. And in turn Christians then spotlight their sexual behaviors as a defense mechanism, rather than looking at their whole person. This impasse will never be breached unless Christians are the first ones to humble themselves.

That starts with acknowledging the GLBT community's perceptions of evangelicalism. Believers are convinced they know what gays and lesbians think, but actually, GLBT people's real thoughts and fears are totally different. This is exactly where the systemic disconnect begins. There are nine main concepts that both the secular and religious GLBT communities think and fear regarding conservative evangelical Christian churches and people.

1. How can I possibly relate to Christians in a church environment?

2. Will Christians always look at me as just gay?

3. Will I be able to be like everyone else in church activities and groups?

4. Do they think that homosexuality is a special sin?

5. Do they believe that I chose to be like this?

6. Do they think that I'm going to hit on them?

7. Do they think that I'm going to abuse their children?

8. Are they scared that I'm going to infect them with an STD or HIV/AIDS?

9. When will I be rejected and kicked out?

There is a striking belief in the inevitability that one, if not all, of these nine reactions will happen at some point if GLBT people were to involve themselves with Christendom. As much as we might even be appalled by this thought process, the GLBT mindset is not any different from many of the common hurdles Americans have as well. Much research has recently been done about the barriers to Christianity, and some of the common findings—anti-gay, too judgmental, hypocritical, won't be able to fit in, too concerned with numbers and demographics instead of spiritual growth—align very closely with the broader scope of the GLBT community's fears as well.[1] The one gaping difference however is that everyday Americans are still a desirable people to have in the religious fold. The same can't be said for gays and lesbians.

Practically speaking, I don't know many GLBT people who would be willing to put themselves out there with all of those nine common risks—including the very real possibility of abandonment time after time. Christians don't give enough credit to the GLBT community for their perseverance and will to find belonging as a child of God while attempting to try to figure out who they are in relation to God sexually, spiritually and socially. These nine fears function as a wall around the GLBT person so he or she won't get hurt. It takes time, patience and trust to break through such walls. The problem has been that the old Christian paradigm was to try and break down all of those walls with a battering ram in one fell swoop—right here, right now. Unfortunately, look where that method has gotten us.

WHAT CAN CHRISTIANS DO?

The Christian community is by and large well intentioned in its interactions with gays and lesbians. We have a tendency, however, to keep making the same mistakes, which end up causing severe harm and reinforce an already negative perception of who we are and what we believe.

Christians must be the first to apologize, and admit that we have wronged people who are gay, lesbian, bisexual and transgender. A bridge cannot be built from just one side of a divide, but the traditional paradigm asks the GLBT community to somehow find their way to the Christian side of the divide before any meaningful contact is made. Until we come to the realization that we don't understand the GLBT community, nothing substantial can occur. My experience has proven that right from the gate Christians can't relate. Unless you have been sexually attracted to someone of the same sex you can never fully grasp, as a heterosexual Christian, what that means. So don't pretend like you know, because that is the quickest way to lose credibility in a GLBT person's mind.

Put yourself in their shoes for a moment and honestly try to imagine the feeling of what it's like to first realize you have a same-sex attraction: the thoughts, questions and issues that all quickly arise without being able to find any definitive answers. Then try to imagine the realization that immediately follows; whether or not that person ever acts out on their same-sex attraction they are inherently cast as deviant to mainline Christianity. Stepping out of what we know in order to comprehend their life from their perspective is the only way we can ultimately begin to learn how to productively reach out and build a bridge.

Christians too easily lose sight of the fact that not everyone takes what we say as genuine. In fact from my experience, the GLBT community's default system is to *never* take *anything* Christians say as genuine. The problem occurs when believers respond to such skepticism by immediately becoming defensive. Peacefulness and productivity never come from a defensive state. Every day I have GLBT people apologize to me for how they acted when they first met me. They were crass, jaded, antagonistic and extremely skeptical until I was able to tangibly prove over a lengthy period of time that I am not the "evil Christian character" they have imbedded in their head.

Too quickly we turn difficult situations on ourselves, interpreting our experience as that of a martyr and concentrating on how to get ourselves out of whatever we've found ourselves in. When my best friends first came out to me I was so fixated on myself, the "why me" questions and how to pretend they never actually "came out" that I forgot to even attempt to try to understand what they were going through. I never thought about the guts it took for them to tell me that they were gay. More importantly, I never thought about what it must have been like for them to live closeted and scared as their best friend unashamedly lived as a Bible-banging homophobe.

It's not about us! It's never been about our life, our situation or what we have to endure. It's about a person exposing their life, staring us in the face, terrified at how we might react. That is a sacred moment, and some of us are fortunate enough to have had the privilege of being intimately involved in the moment a person chooses to trust us with their secret identity, their secret curse, their secret sin or whatever their secret might be.

Very few times are these truly sacred moments shared between people. "I have cancer," "We lost the baby," "I'm getting married," "I am gay"—all brief moments in time when a person chooses to speak their life-changing revelation out loud. Participating in such a moment is an eternal bond regardless of what happens from that moment forward. If we desecrate that trust and violate that moment by turning the focus onto ourselves, we have lost much of what our faith allows us to be.

Even if Christians don't agree with the GLBT community or what they might stand for, believers in Christ are supposed to know how to find real empathy for those who are going through things we can never understand. When we get our first glimpse of that genuine empathy, let it soak in until it becomes a real expression of our appreciation of what GLBT people face twenty-four hours a day, seven days a week.

The GLBT community shouldn't have to demand that from Christians. We should demand it of ourselves as faithful stewards of the responsibility that they have given us by letting a straight, conservative Christian into their world. Let us then learn and listen and validate the reality of their stories as to what did actually happen in their life. Validation is different from affirmation, and it is an essential starting point to take gay people at their word. The more skeptical we are, the more we doubt the validity of a gay's or lesbian's life, the more shallow and ineffective our relationships become.

2

We Are Not Your Project

Sexual Behavior Is Gay Identity

Christians tend to perceive themselves as morally superior to GLBT people, based on the belief that the Bible allows only three options for connecting faith and sexuality: be heterosexual,[1] be celibate or live in sin. Once Christians have presented these three options to a gay person, most consider their job effectively complete as it's now up to the gay person to either embrace or reject this truth.

Yet gays and lesbians hear these three options as a definitive challenge, and therefore feel their only recourse is to suit up for battle. When it comes to identity, sexual behavior and sexuality, gays and lesbians have a unique filtration system. Our understanding of change, celibacy and sin is oppressive and destructive when run through their filter. Much of the time, GLBT people just write off the rest of the conversation, and thus what began as a potentially intriguing conversation ends up as a heated debate.

We miss out on soul-stirring dialogues when we fail to openly enter into an unnerving conversation. In effect, without realizing it we are sabotaging these relationships one at a time.

SAME-SEX SEXUAL BEHAVIOR

Socially and politically, much of what the gay, lesbian, bisexual and transgender community believes in and fights is related to their sexual behavior. It is one of the main characteristics that sets GLBT people apart from everyone else, and so it's also one of the main keys to unlocking a significant portion of the GLBT mindset.

Over the years I have had many gay people tell me that if someone were to take away their sexual behavior, they would be taking away all they are as people. Same-sex sexual behavior *is* the source of the inherent disconnect between conservative Christianity and gays and lesbians. But we have never tried to thoroughly dig in and peacefully dialogue with pragmatic understanding about same-sex sexual behavior for the simple reason that it *is* the cause of our inherent disconnect. One of the most important topics to them should also be one of the most important topics for heterosexual Christians to learn about and try to wrap our heads around from their perspective. And yet we don't.

We have no problem wrestling with apologetics for people of different ethnicities and cultures that are totally removed from ours. Christians diligently study other belief systems and incarnationally move into the neighborhoods of people with different beliefs, join their groups, attend their events and partake in their daily life, reveling in the unique opportunity to engage what we don't know. But Christians do none of those things for the GLBT community. In fact, when my wife and I tell people that we have never had same-sex attractions and purposefully live (and plan to raise a family) in the GLBT community of Boystown in Chicago, we regularly receive strange looks. At every church I visit, at least one person comes to me on the side and asks me if my story is really true—if I actually did *those* things with *those* people and went to *those* places.

The Christian community has only ever known one way to handle same-sex sexual behavior: take a stand and keep a distance. Productive dialogue comes from cognitive insight and can only be accomplished through an incarnational posture of humility and living as a learner.

BEHAVIOR VERSUS IDENTITY?

Sin of any kind is, theologically, an offense against God's created intent because it's a behavior that violates our identity as creatures that bear his image. The doctrine of the Fall contends that because of such offenses, human beings will ultimately receive a sentence of death. Most important, though, the doctrine of salvation counteractively asserts that Jesus' act on the cross atones for our sins and frees us to embrace our identity as a child of God.

Therefore when it comes to Christian behavior and identity, each is understood as independent of the other: what we do is not necessarily who we are; and who we are is not necessarily what we do. New covenant faith tells us that we are covered by the grace of our Father through his Son, Jesus Christ. Although we are not perfect, what we do—whether good or bad, well intentioned or not—does not eternally define us or affect our identity as that child of God.

The GLBT community's filtration system, however, is once again different from our own in how they relate to same-sex attraction and sexual behavior. Since the GLBT person's mindset attests that same-sex sexual behavior is the dominating characteristic that sets them apart from everyone else, their sexual behavior *is* who they are. For many GLBT people it becomes their defining characteristic, and as such, their same-sex sexual behavior equals their identity.

As a result, when gay and lesbian sexual behavior is challenged or questioned, they perceive their entire being as a person—their whole identity—as being under attack. When this occurs they feel as though their distinct individuality as a GLBT person has been effectively negated. What we may have thought was an offer of help, of insight into what the Bible commands, has instead become the epicenter of Christianity's assault on homosexuality. Contextually, Christians might not agree with these associations. But taking them as a legitimate part of who the GLBT community sees themselves to be will dramatically assist us in our ability to constructively enter into their world from their perspective.

SEXUALITY'S INFINITE CONTINUUM

There are hundreds of books and academic research articles that claim they have found the final, definitive answer in proving or disproving that same-sex attraction is either genetic or environmental. My intent is to do neither. This is a debate that can never be solved. One side will endlessly search for a gay gene or a way to prove that their orientation is not a lifestyle choice. The other side will continue to research a behavioral choice and ex-gay position. And each community will continue to demand that the other concede their thesis. This is what I call sexuality's infinite continuum.

Sexuality's infinite continuum persists because both communities are working off of a false model of "the ideal situation"—that the other side will eventually realize their mistake and give up everything they have been fighting for. Neither community's ideal situation can happen because neither the Christian nor GLBT community will ever let it happen. Neither side is going to give up the genetics-environmental debate in the foreseeable future, and instead of continuing to verbally and scientifically abuse each other, I propose a new paradigm: it is possible to disagree and yet still peacefully listen, learn and dialogue so that something significant can happen for the kingdom.

In general, Christians' default belief system is environmental. Because of certain social, familial or predisposed genetic factors in combination with outside influences that occur during one's developmental stages, the theory goes, one's sexual identity and gender development becomes skewed and therefore the person is not able to experience an "ideal" opposite-sex intimate relationship. I know many Christians who enjoy playing psychologist—talking to GLBT people to figure out if they had an absentee dad or a domineering mom, played with either Barbies or G.I. Joes at three years old, or experienced some kind of sexual abuse in their youth.

What this means is that, in the Christian community's eyes, the person who has a same-sex attraction—whether they act on it or not—is inherently damaged because of their uncontrollable circumstances

as a developing child. Add this to the reality that same-sex attractions—whether acted on or not—automatically cast a person as deviant to mainline Christianity, and all of a sudden Christianity is no
longer the come-as-you-are culture we are supposed to be. Now, we
might argue that *everyone* is inherently damaged by sin. True. But
mention to a Christian that you are sexually attracted to the opposite
sex and you likely won't be hit with questions about your mom, your
dad or the intimate details about your sexual history.

It is much easier to believe that all GLBT people either had a very
bad family life or were sexually abused because Christians are then
excused from facing the unexplainable reason as to why God would
allow someone to be given such a lot in life. Our naiveté gives the
GLBT community a useful rallying cry. Christians are caricatured
as stereotypical, ignorant, uncaring, anti-gay bigots, whom GLBT
people are rightly repulsed and frightened by.

ABUSE AND ITS IMPACT

On the other hand, developmental growth can be seriously affected
by sexual or mental abuse. There are indeed GLBT people who have
experienced abuse, and many in the broader gay community do not
want to talk about it. But abused GLBT people tell me the reason
they don't want to talk about their past with Christians is because
Christians are already expecting that story. The Christian expectation does nothing more than further invalidate a gay or lesbian person's worth and existence.

GLBT victims of abuse think Christians consider their wretched
past as "normal" to the gay experience. But no matter who it is—
Christian, non-Christian, gay or straight—abuse is anything but
normal. Abuse in and of itself will not directly produce an out-
wardly identifiable GLBT identity; rather, it is the intricate and parallel internalizations that transpire over time which become their
story, their journey, their persona. But too many gays and lesbians
are unwilling to share their secrets, pain and hidden terrors with us
for the simple reason that they anticipate we will respond to them

not as victims of abuse but as just one more person whose abuse made them gay.

One of the first people I ever met through The Marin Foundation was Maddie. One fall evening she knocked on my door and wanted to take a walk. We were strolling down a bike path near her apartment when we happened on an empty park bench and sat down. It was only a brief moment before she started to hysterically cry and tell me something she said she had never told anyone else.

One summer when Maddie was nine years old her dad calmly brought her into the bathroom in their basement and chained her to the toilet. The chain was so tightly locked around her ankles and waist that she couldn't move; she had no other option than to just lay down next to the toilet on the dirty bathroom floor.

"If you ever tell anybody I'll kill you," Maddie's dad would remind her.

Each day she would yell, cry and plead for him to unlock her. He would come down to the basement and toss her a tin plate with some food scraps on it, not caring that Maddie's ankles were cut up from the chains and her waist was raw with infected wounds as the skin was slowly scraped off.

After three months of being locked up with no explanation, her dad apologized and let her out to return to fourth grade that following fall. "I wanted to believe his apology," she told me, "until he started raping me."

By the time the sexual abuse stopped Maddie was fourteen years old and her life had been taken away from her. What Maddie told me next was something I never thought I'd hear: "I'm not attracted to girls, but no man will ever touch me ever again." She is so scared of grown men that she chooses to be a lesbian.

Can you blame Maddie for those feelings? As I always do when I don't know what else to do I just sat and listened to her some more. I kept thinking that she was right; nobody *could* take away what her father did to her—except our Father. Although Maddie can't see God and doesn't know God personally, she can feel him, and she can see me sitting there as his representative, participating in her life without rules or judgments or religious commentary.

Reflecting on that time spent with Maddie, I'm reminded of the comfort Job received from his friends when they served as silent witnesses mourning with him. It was when those friends started preaching that everything went south. There are just times in life when words, any words, are inadequate. One of the most important things we can do in those times is to understand our role. I have learned that much of my time spent in relationship with the GLBT community revolves around living as that silent witness—being sturdy in my faith and being with them at the time they need God's comfort the most.

Whenever I hear something new I like to ask as many other people as I can about it to see if they feel the same. So every time I talk to a GLBT person who, by their own accord, opens up about a sexually abusive past, I ask them about their thoughts on their attractions to people of the same sex. Jennifer was physically abused by her father in high school; Thom was molested by his neighbor for five years; Cynthia was fondled by her cousin from age seven to age thirteen; Rich was raped by his uncle from elementary school to high school. Each one of them today says that they choose to be part of the GLBT community not because they feel they were born gay but because of their abuse.

More people than I expected felt this way, but by no means a significant percentage of the GLBT people I know. Maddie, Jennifer, Thom, Cynthia and Rich are a small number of the broader GLBT community. Even though these stories exist, we must be careful not to generalize abuse as an explanation of why GLBT people are the way they are—as research suggests that on average only 7 to 15 percent of the GLBT community was sexually abused in their youth.

Christians must take the responsibility to make a mental shift away from the "sexually abused default system" for the sake of those who we will encounter in the future. We can't blend each of their individual lives together to make them a single, homogenous group. If you look past the stereotypical caricature of what you think gay is, your eyes will open to a new GLBT community—a community that longs for our Father's eternity just as we do.

WHAT HAS OUR RESPONSE BEEN?

I have heard from many different Christian churches and organizations around the United States that everything the GLBT community does or believes is just a ploy to normalize same-sex sexual behaviors. Yet I strongly believe that the Christian community has done more to equate sexual behavior with sexual identity among the GLBT community than they have themselves. Instead of presenting life as an opportunity to become something spiritually new in Christ, the Christian community continues to fight against the hand that we're actually dealing them.

On a larger scale Christians have given the gay community the impression that only their sexual behavior is worth discussing, labeling GLBT people as nothing more than a dysfunctional set of sexual attractions and behaviors rather than whole persons with unique stories to tell. Our relationships to them become muddled with same-sex sexual behaviors first and foremost, instead of letting Jesus unequivocally lead the way.

A gay friend of mine recently told me a story about an experience he had at work. His story clearly illustrates how Christians continue to focus on same-sex sexual behavior and its potential pitfalls as the driving force in how we reduce our outlook of, and relationships with, gays and lesbians:

I had lunch again with Sam on Tuesday—the guy from my office who goes to [a conservative church]. I've gotten to know him really well over our many lunches, and I was at the point that I thought earlier that morning I would tell him what I am all about since I really have no time for superficial relationships. But during lunch, out of nowhere he says, "My hometown has a very large gay population." I asked why. He said,

"Because there is a pretty decent hospital there so they all come there to *die!*" I asked in shock, "From what?" He said, "Of course, AIDS." Needless to say I didn't tell him anything about me from that point forward. He can go on thinking I am just "one of the guys" and he will *never* know the real me or ever be my friend. This is *why* I can't be friends with Christians—they just *don't get it!* I have to lie too much and work too hard at being something I'm not to be loved or even a friend to a Christian. That is sad, so very, very sad.

What we might think is an insignificant conversation with a person—any person—has the very real potential to shape that individual's outlook on what Christianity is, who Christians are, and how Christians handle their faith and life. Over the years many people in the GLBT community have told me about the lasting impact from a conversation they once had with a Christian—a conversation that Christian acquaintance probably doesn't even remember. That might not be fair, but it's a reality. Yet the good news is that our God is sovereign over reality. So what do we, as followers of that sovereign God, do to overcome that situation?

WHAT CHRISTIANS CAN DO:
DON'T CUT THE CONVERSATION SHORT

First we have to start moving past our default responses toward the GLBT community. I am not asking Christians to change their beliefs, nor am I asking them to change their foundational understanding of Scripture. We must, however, acknowledge how our three traditional options—heterosexuality, celibacy or a life of sin—are received by GLBT people. We have been too wrapped up in planning the communication of our truth by cooking up contingency plans for potential rebuttals that we have forgotten to think relationally. Looking for opportunities to build trust will inevitably remove some of the fears and obvious obstacles we face. Throughout my Christian life I have learned that building trust is a means to transform confusion into clarity. The driving force behind the conceptualization of how we traditionally communicate with GLBT people stems from the uncertainty of how to productively talk about same-sex sexual behaviors. Insecurities will overtake a clear mind and cause nothing more than a bland regurgitation of the same three options that gays and lesbians view as an attack—and thus, the negative cycle continues. Christians struggle with the tendency to put all of their eggs in one basket because of the constant pressure to seal the gospel deal in one shot.

Unfortunately that thought process is stifling what should be some of our most intriguing and vital conversations about what most gays and lesbians see as the whole basis for their identity. I have found through personal interactions with a wide range of GLBT people, as well as through the scientific research conducted by The Marin Foundation, that their community has a very high religiosity. To understand that is to have a place of common ground, and the more we rely on conversation stoppers the more complicated we make the spiritual quest we wish for everyone.

Christians talk too much because we really don't know what to say and how to say it. It's time to pay more attention to living out what we believe instead of always trying to say it.

DON'T TAKE THE BAIT

Some gays and lesbians tell me they bait Christians, trying to lead them into a no-win debate about gay sexual behavior and identity. Why would someone do that? GLBT people believe that if they bring up the hot topics first they will be able to control the conversation and protect themselves from being hurt, embarrassed or segregated. Ultimately if Christians fall back into the old paradigm of engagement and prove their suspicions right, we give gays and lesbians the right to categorize us as more Bible-banging homophobes who don't deserve their time of day.

When we hear these polarizing debates start to arise, then, instead of bracing ourselves for a debate we should take a step back and assess the situation. Always err on the side of meekness in spirit and conduct. Research suggests that it's not nearly as likely that the gay, lesbian, bisexual or transgender we talk to has been abused as it is that they

- have been hurt in their past by a Christian
- have a negative perception of Christianity
- have the nine-layered wall already in place
- are anticipating criticism about their sexuality and sexual behaviors
- are already braced for a fight

I find it helpful to be honest and open when I sense that I'm being baited. I make it clear that I'm not there to fight or attempt to convince them that their belief system is wrong. I indicate that I'd be interested in learning from them what they believe. This diffuses a potentially volatile situation, and it earns much needed credibility in their eyes. It also opens the door to a two-way, pressure-free conversation, and opens up our relationship to spiritually intimate levels we never thought possible.

LOVE THE SINNER, HATE THE SIN

One of the most difficult juxtapositions Christians find themselves in is how to balance a relationship with a GLBT person while maintaining their convictions about traditional biblical mandates for sexuality. This is the number one reason that keeps believers from entering into potentially deep spiritual relationships with searching GLBT people. More often than not we just default to the well-known phrase "love the sinner, hate the sin."

Among gays and lesbians, "love the sinner, hate the sin" is the most disdained phrase in the Christian vocabulary. If behavior equals identity, then hating gay sexual behavior is the same thing as hating the gay person. The most common rebuttal they use to counter that slogan is Jesus' words regarding judgment in Matthew

7, where he speaks about the plank in our own eye and the speck in our brother's. "How can Christians pick this one sin and make it greater than all the rest? The Bible also says not to _____ [for example, "eat crab"]. Straight people _____ and yet are still accepted." As the Barna Group discovered in research commissioned by the Fermi Project, this logic has earned Christians a reputation for being extremely hypocritical and unrightfully judgmental.

The easiest way we can start to change these negative perceptions is to remove "love the sinner, hate the sin" from our vocabulary. Clever catch phrases that try to make Christianity accessible to the masses don't translate to all different populations. As soon as we drop the notion of loving the sinner and hating the sin, the pressure is then off of us to drag a GLBT person from their current "corrupted state" to our "holy state," just as the pressure is off of the GLBT person to continually build up their defenses to try to guard against the slogans that hurt them time and again.

3

Stigma, Shame and Politics

The GLBT Experience in the Broader Culture

We were sitting on plush cushions in a dimly lit room at a sushi restaurant in one of Chicago's trendy neighborhoods. Whenever Arnold and I meet he likes to take me to one of the city's newest hip restaurants. He uses his money, nicely tailored clothes and political clout to overshadow the shame that emanates from his tortured mind. The internal battle that he has had to struggle with and suffer through for the last ten years has disintegrated any remains of what could have been a young, thriving life. Each time we part ways I am left squirming as I see Arnold join a long line of people who've become a casualty of the gay stigma that engulfs their entire being.

The GLBT community feels a constant unnamed pressure from both sides—an invisible Christian ideal that they can't see themselves living up to, and an overt push from the gay-friendly culture to just "come out" and be OK with it. Neither option seems achievable to many people who have a same-sex attraction, so they are left with no home and no sense of support. A large portion of these people eventually try to force themselves to fit into one of these unnatural categories just so they can belong somewhere. And most of the time that category is not the Christian ideal.

Arnold feels the burden of having to be the multiple people that his gay acquaintances, his coworkers, his family and his faith all want him to be. Yet he has lost track of the stories, the lies and the drive to keep it all going at such an efficient level. Over the years, I have known of a lot of people like Arnold who have lost all of their identity and self-worth; they feel as though they are living a constant lie, trying to be whoever the person they are talking to wants them to be.

Within any social context that I research, read about or am involved with regarding the GLBT community, three driving forces carry the capacity to turn bright, spiritually minded people into their generation's version of the Stepford wives: stigma, shame and politics.

All of us have our own spheres of influence, mostly through our circle of friends, family and those we interact with on a daily basis. Each of these spheres, in the context of both a secular and religious culture, have become reductionist in nature. Entertainment programming, particularly reality television, has efficiently reduced culture into microscopic minority subgroups of what the world is. For nineteen seasons MTV's *Real World* has featured a stable of recurrent characters: the militant African American, the flamboyant gay person, at least one hot blonde-haired woman and a smattering of athletic muscle-bound males of varying ethnicities. *American Idol,* on the other hand, continues to pit subgroups in the music industry against each other: the rocker versus the naive sweet girl with a huge voice, the country wannabe versus the teenyboppin' heartthrob, and so on.

Such reductions are happening in churches as well. Which church in my local community is politically connected to the mayor, alderman or city council? What postmodern, emergent church can I wear ragged jeans and a T-shirt to? Which church has the cool, socially in-tune small groups? Who are the people in my church connected to the lead pastor, the board of elders and the high-roller donors of influence? Who "fellowships" while golfing at exclusive clubs during the day and eats dinner at the places I could only wish to get a reservation at?

This current framework has entrenched these newly formed minority subgroups into neatly sectioned-off boxes—each of which has been given their own little space to function. Although more pronounced today, the same deconstruction can be seen as far back as the Israelites in the Old Testament. Minority groups—whether by force, by choice or by attrition—eventually acculturate to the majority. Within the majority lies a sense of normalization that includes a further reach of influence and power.

No matter how many times God warned the Israelites to keep themselves set apart from the surrounding nations—that he was all they ever needed—they chose to intermarry and give their sons and daughters away because they wanted so deeply to weave themselves into the fabric of their culture. Soong-Chan Rah, a seminary professor at North Park University, speaks and writes extensively on the "white captivity" of today's evangelical church. He believes the cultural position of power that comes with Caucasian skin has dramatically, and many times negatively, shaped Asian Americans' yearning to assimilate. Just the same the broader GLBT community as a minority group feels they've also been held captive by the power of the evangelical church and its overwhelming pressure to fall in line.

STIGMA AND SHAME IN MAINSTREAM CULTURE

Current data, depending on the source, estimates that gays, lesbians, bisexuals and transgenders account for somewhere between 1 and 7 percent of the American population. An overwhelmingly larger percentage of the population—around 36 percent—identify themselves as traditionally conservative, Bible-believing Christians. Although throughout the centuries America has lost a significant portion of its original biblical moorings, Christianity is still numerically the number one religion, and therefore has a significant channel to influence culture. Just look to the unexpected results of the November 2008 Proposition 8 vote that overturned California's legalization of same-sex marriage.

The GLBT community sees itself as one of the many minority casualties of Christendom. This feeling unleashes a cultural stigma that today drives much of what gays and lesbians fight for. Stigma is a mode of perception—a culturally felt expression of dominance from one person or group over another. Stigma, however, goes far beyond just the intersection between religion and homosexuality. It is also prominently displayed in many other public arenas.

A good friend of mine has AIDS. He got infected while completing his undergraduate work at an Ivy League school. After years of having an undetectable HIV viral load while on medication, in 2005 his immune cell count rapidly dropped over a period of a few months. Now he dreads going to bed each night because he knows all too well the familiar burning pain, nausea and intoxicating feeling that come from taking that one large, awful pill that keeps him alive.

He used his brilliant Ivy League mind to rocket himself to the highest corporate levels within the world of technology. Over nearly twenty-five years he advanced his way through a nationally recognizable company to become the chief technological officer. Work is his life; he stays at the office as long as he possibly can because it's his only respite. When he goes home, the only thing waiting for him is that cocktailed pill. Too often he questions whether or not it's worth the torture just to keep living a miserable existence.

My friend's family is ashamed of him; they think he deserves what he got. His gay friends don't know he has AIDS; he doesn't want to scare them off. His employees assumed that his debilitating illness is cancer, not AIDS—that was, until someone in his human resources department made the biggest mistake of their career: accidentally leaving his insurance paperwork in the copy machine.

One day he was sitting at his desk, catching up on everything he missed during a recent two-month medical leave. A pregnant employee walked into his office, and he looked up and smiled before noticing that she was tensely cringing with closed fists. She suddenly pointed her index finger directly at him and yelled as loud as she possibly could: "I will not ever work another day here until he is removed! He has AIDS and he's going to infect my baby! He has AIDS!"

What happened then is hardly believable. Security came in and removed him. The next day the executive committee that he is a part of met without him. Allowing him no input into their decision, they relocated his office to their company's old building down the street. His options were to be the only employee in that now-abandoned space, or accept a buyout under the pretenses of "losing control of his staff."

How quickly things change when people know the truth. "You tend to get complacent," he told me, "because you think being gay or having HIV/AIDS is no longer a big deal until you get smacked in the face with a strong dose of reality that nothing has really changed." No one cared enough to warn him that everyone in the office found out about his condition. No one cared enough to tell him that a certain group of employees were scared to get infected and no longer wanted to work for him. Twenty-five years of loyally working twelve-to-fourteen-hour days led him to a choice between isolation and abandonment or hush money.

My friend felt betrayed and took neither of their options, staying exactly where he was to make his colleagues face what they tried to force upon him. I was smiling on the other end of the phone when he told me, because he had finally realized that his life is just as valuable as yours or mine. To his company and those employees it didn't matter that he had become a believer and worshiped regularly at a local church. It didn't matter to them that he was celibate. It didn't matter to them that he obsessively disinfected everything he touched (even though HIV can never be acquired in such a fashion). It didn't matter to them that he walked in total self-hated before God's forgiveness ever graced his life. But to me, and for the first time to him, it did matter. Eventually an investigation began into how my friend's company handled his situation. Only time will tell how it is resolved. No matter what the outcome, the damage has already been done.

Andy Crouch, author of the book *Culture Making,* says that Christians don't change culture by critiquing culture. They change culture by making culture.[1] When even the secular mainstream casts gay people as deviant and horrid, the Christian community is presented with an opportunity to change the culture by making a new one: offering hope and compassion to a people who have been burdened with a thick dose of stigma and shame in all aspects of their life.

STIGMA AND SHAME IN HISTORICAL GAY CULTURE

GLBT people have their own individual stories, but they also have the communal stories of the challenges they've had to face as an oppressed people. Cultural experiences shape not only a people's mindset but their subsequent actions and reactions. A lot of time, energy and money have been spent by the GLBT community highlighting "religious injustices." And yet although that might be valid to their experience within many sects of Christendom, I believe that their struggle within the broader mainstream culture has been intentionally forgotten.

By all accounts the modern era of the GLBT community began on June 28, 1969, when a group of gay, lesbian, bisexual and transgender people rioted in the streets of New York City. Police had attempted to raid a Mafia-owned, underground gay bar called Stonewall Inn. For the first time gays and lesbians banded together in a public way to resist what had become frequent shakedowns by undercover police who continually threatened public arrest and "outing" if they were not paid off. GLBT historians call those Riots the birthplace of gay rights. It's a little-known fact that originally, all of the gay pride parades around the country were held at the same time during the last weekend in June in order to commemorate the stand at Stonewall Inn.

A year and a half ago two gray-haired African American women came up to me after a workshop I conducted at a New York City event. Louise and Mary Ann have been together for almost fifty years; and on June 28, 1969, they were at Stonewall Inn when the undercover police began the raid. This was the first time I had met anyone who was directly involved. In all of my studies on the Riot I have never come across anything dissecting religion and spirituality from a GLBT perspective dating back to that crucial period in their history, and I was dying to ask them all about it. I quickly offered to take them out to eat, and they were more than happy to join me.

Like an impatient kid, as soon as we sat down I blurted my thoughts out loud and asked if they ever saw God or religion as a basis for anything that preceded the Riot. Louise said, "Undercover police raided Stonewall very frequently. They didn't do it because of God, just like politicians don't make laws because of God. They wanted our money, not our faith.

"I don't believe that society casts us off because of God. What is different makes people uncomfortable, and in order to hurt us, they needed a cause. I believe religion was the cause they—and many others—decided to stand behind to cover the real issues: the issue that my sexuality makes people squirm."

Mary Ann added: "We fought because what else did we have to lose? We didn't have any dignity, they took our money every raid, and we lived in fear. You can't live like that. We had nowhere else to go. We were stuck in a violent cycle."

From that moment on I began to look at Stonewall, and ultimately the Gay Pride Parade that came as a result, differently. The parades have become something dramatically different from their original intent. The day after the parades are concluded, newspapers across the country always seem to have a full-page color picture of a very large, boa-wearing, cross-dressing man dancing on a stripper pole on the top of a float. But to actually spend time with people who were involved in the Stonewall Riots puts a new perspective on the historical-cultural context of the Pride Parade and what it means to the first-generation GLBT community. What Christians see as a blatant in-your-face act was originally intended to peacefully remember those who stood up and fought for the first time against GLBT social and cultural oppression.

This new understanding let me realize that cultural expression takes shape in unique ways through the experiences of the hearts and souls of those involved. As Christians are able to change our posture and approach toward gay culture—and our understanding of gay history—the shame, stigma and politics that color Christian-GLBT relations can be gradually replaced with honest conversations about heartfelt convictions without one group feeling the strong urge to run from the other.

STIGMA AND SHAME IN POLITICAL CULTURE

I began my immersion only thirty-one years after the Stonewall Riots, and thus, the first generation of the modern GLBT community is still leading the organizations that currently shape the social and political opinions of the gay world. They remember what life was like before there was any protection or ability to live as an out gay or lesbian person. In the eras before Stonewall the cultural stigma surrounding GLBT issues was so pervasive that in many cities around the country any one of the following actions could have easily resulted in an immediate arrest a fine, jail time or admission into a mental institution without a hearing:

- two people of the same sex showing affection for one another in public by holding hands, hugging or kissing
- two people of the same sex dancing with one another
- bars or clubs serving alcohol to GLBT persons
- publically declaring one's sexual orientation as gay, lesbian, bisexual or transgender

Even as recent as 2002 there were still fourteen states that upheld the sodomy law, and in Idaho, one could land a lifetime sentence in jail for engaging in gay sexual behaviors. George, an older gay man from New York City, works for a GLBT activist group. He told me one afternoon over lunch,

> Politics have changed everything. The fight has become different. It's no longer about dignity but rather about changing laws to validate us as people. I know I'm a person; I don't need

a law to validate that. But the younger group doesn't know what it was like to live in the world we had to live in. They take for granted what we fought for. They have lost the big picture: we were constantly scared of the police and people seriously hurting us.

George also has an interesting take on the religious debate. "I feel religion has become a scapegoat for us. We know it's there, we know they hate us, but they're not going to ever change. Instead of giving them more relevance let's focus on what we can change— the legal system."

From George's perspective, Christian faith and beliefs have no cultural impact. To those involved in the political battle, Jesus Christ is not God's only Son who came to die to forgive all of their sins but rather a rationalization for subjugation. Cultural relevance is the key to systemic change, and if Christians are thought of as dead or irrelevant we have no tangible means to then make a systemic difference within culture.

While at an event I was invited to in Chicago I met a high-ranking official from the Gay and Lesbian Alliance Against Defamation (GLAAD). I didn't know how many more opportunities I would have to talk one-on-one in private with such a person, so I asked him why their organization, and others who fight for the same things, are so fervently opposed to evangelical Christianity. He likened the situation to a boxing match and said, "When we have been backed into a corner for so long, the only way for us to get out is to come out swinging."

In seminary I was told by one of my professors to never use sports analogies or illustrations; a lot of people either don't care or don't understand. Nevertheless, this GLBT leader had just succinctly articulated the oldest and still the most effective rallying cry that a sports team can use to bond together: "Us against the world—we are the only ones who believe in us, and we will prove everyone else wrong until they start to believe as well."

People think that mindset is entertaining in movies: compelling, as we root for the underdog. And yet in real life both Christians and the GLBT community are imagining themselves in the same role: each as the underdog who has to fight their way out of the corner. Both believe they are David and the other is Goliath. Two oppressed mindsets fighting each other will never be able to win the same battle.

SHAME AND CHURCH CULTURE: VIEW FROM INSIDE

Over the years shame has been passed down through secular culture surrounding gays and lesbians. That shame has also imbedded itself in the core of the church. The overarching stigma felt by GLBT people with the church is continually brought to light by the ingrained cultural psyche that shame is supposed to be the inherent, default feeling for all who have a same-sex attraction—Christian or non-Christian.

The major problem with this association is that it leaves no room for a journey, as shame continues to smother what could potentially be a thriving relationship with God. The conclusion has always been forced ahead of the story. There are no clearer examples of this than a series of introductory emails I have received from two different people who were searching for a release from their internal tortures. Their stories, and the questions that emerged from them, have dramatically affected how I look at faith, shame and the church. I struggle to find all of the answers. Despite how uncomfortable I've become, I do know these are the lives the God of my faith would have sought. Then so do I.

I received an email from a man who, I came to find out afterward, was planning on killing himself. After hearing me on the radio he decided to send along this suicide note even though we had never met—he didn't feel any of his family, friends or church would have taken it seriously.

Had someone had the courage to tell me that promiscuity of any type is wrong, that it is OK to not marry or being gay is not the end of the world then I might have been spared a great deal of trauma and pain in my life. My past is not pretty but I don't know that many that are. For me, it isn't about making it, but is about survival and *truly knowing peace*. . . . It is painful to think that people find it easy to shun us—some of us actually do have good hearts that can be worth salvaging. . . .

There are all kinds of medals given out for going to Africa to help with AIDS and for dealing with "respectable" illnesses but the stigma attached to being gay is as prevalent today as ever. How sad. This *is* the reason I don't go to services—I can't find a temple or church that is really eager to allow me to be honest with what I face on a daily basis. It has always been as though I was supposed to already be "fixed" just because I showed up at services. Anyway I have reached a point of hopelessness because there really is no one with a true heart to help.

Do our churches really give the impression that GLBT people have to be fixed before they are allowed to attend? Can we give love to (and be loved by) those without pretty pasts? Can we allow for God's redemptive cycle to work in people's lives without ever knowing the ending? Or is his assessment right?

The knowledge of love and shame, and how we teach them to students in Christian universities and congregants in Christian churches, runs deeper than just someone on the outside looking for help.

Andrew,

I heard you a while ago and I was so impressed because you have such compassion for the gay community and treat them with such dignity and respect (something the body of Christ rarely ever does). I know you're based in Chicago and I live in a different part of the country, but I am a Christian woman who is married with a daughter, and I struggle with lesbian tendencies. I live in . . . an ultra conservative evangelical town. My husband works at [a major Christian university] and I feel I could endanger his employment were I to seek "help" in a public way. My church is not known as a place where anyone ever sins or struggles with anything.

I just got out of rehab for alcoholism and I have used alcohol for years to make all these feelings go away. My husband does know I have these thoughts but has no idea how much I struggle. I do not feel I can go to my church and I do not know where else to turn. I fear for my salvation.

My son died in 1996 and my daughter is disabled and can't function in any "normal" capacity. I fear this was God's punishment for my sexual sins of the past. I only want to glorify God and be delivered from all of this because I fear what punishments will happen next. Can you help me please?

Can someone be married, love Christ, by their own admission struggle with same-sex attraction, and yet still be a person of worth and dignity? This sister believes that her son was killed and her daughter is handicapped because of her same-sex attractions! And nobody has told her otherwise—including her husband whose job is to teach the next generation of evangelical pastors. What have we done? Or more aptly, what have we not done that even from within our own walls there is no room for the broken?

Church is a place to give rest to your soul, a place of gathering where anyone should be able to come and involve themselves with a community of believers who are joined by a common faith in the Lord Almighty. Church is believers—transparent, real and raw. Church is a lifetime of discovery as people brace themselves against their neighbor so both are able to stand and walk together. And yet there are still churches around this country with no sinners. I understand that there will always be people who feel intimidated and overwhelmed in church, but we must do everything we possibly can to rectify an image of perfection that no one can live up to, from the lead pastor on down. This woman's plea for help is a clear reminder to all of us of who we're to be with each surrounding brother and sister throughout our place of worship. Feelings of faith, love, shame and stigma are formed in the context of how we relate to one another, even inside our own Christian families and circles.

WHAT CHRISTIANS CAN DO: WORDS MATTER

I was having breakfast with a lesbian who works with people on how to communicate to the media about the GLBT community, and the first thing she said to me was to never use the word *homosexual.* I had never heard that before. I didn't understand why I wasn't supposed to use it and why it was looked upon as so negative. When I asked she explained that the word *homosexual* has only been used as a derogatory biblical term. Since the mainstream GLBT community has traditionally looked at the Bible as a tool of oppression, hearing the word *homosexual* sets off a domino effect of associations: homosexual = Bible = Christian = fundamentalism = anti-gay = anti-me. Furthermore, many in the GLBT community are pleasantly surprised when they meet a Christian who doesn't call them a homosexual.

Have you ever heard anyone who is gay or lesbian refer to themselves or their friends as homosexuals? Is there any coincidence why you haven't? The word *homosexual* is offensive to someone who is gay, lesbian, bisexual or transgender. So instead use words like *gay, lesbian, GLBT, gay and lesbian community.* The most frequent question I get from Christians when I explain this rationale is, "Isn't this the same as conforming to their wishes and doesn't this mean we are playing into their hands?" Let me ask you this question: how do you connect with people whose life experience is significantly different from yours—a business executive, perhaps, or a hip-hop cultured youth, a porn star, an athlete? I can tell you this much: probably not by offending them. The simplest way to diffuse tension with a person from the GLBT community is to recognize their feelings and triggers, and work within those boundaries.

Last summer I was walking down the main street in Boystown in Chicago. A gay man I didn't know stopped me and told me that a week earlier a Christian woman he works with came up to him and said she was sorry for calling him a homosexual all these years. He teared up as he told me that his coworker had taken some of The Marin Foundation's classes for the Christian community. "I have never had anyone apologize to me before for calling me a homosexual. I never realized how much it would impact me. It is something I never thought would happen and it meant the world to me. I look at her totally different because to say that she must have really cared." He then gave me a quick, somewhat awkward hug and ran across the street and started walking in the other direction like nothing had happened.

A week later I got an email from his female coworker. She told me that as she apologized he began to cry at his desk and thanked her for trying to understand.

I never knew one little apology and an omission of one word would give me such an opportunity to talk about God. He can't stop asking me questions. I guess he feels safe now.

Not using the word *homosexual* is not normalizing same-sex behavior, as some conservative activists think it to be. Prior to this section that word hasn't appeared in this book one time, and you probably haven't even noticed. Though I have used the word *homosexuality* it carries a very different cultural relevance than the label of *homosexual*. It's not a big deal to us to either use or not use *homosexual*, but it sure is a big deal to the GLBT community. And if it's a big deal to them, it's a big deal to me too.

ACTIONS MATTER

Years ago when my friends came out to me there was no one I could turn to to help me navigate my immersion experience. I felt weighed down because I knew I was blindly walking into a world I had no idea about. I didn't know what to expect and I didn't know how people were going to react to my presence. All I wanted was some sense of normalcy. Retrospectively, three general points would have greatly helped me traverse this new GLBT terrain.

First, Christians have to get past their own major issues regarding the GLBT community (this will be explored in chapter eight). The last thing anyone wants to do is feed themselves to the wolves. There is something special about walking by faith, but we need to be smart about it. It's counterproductive and even arrogant to think we can help, listen to or learn from anyone else while not being able to get past our own hurdles. The best step for someone who is extremely uncomfortable with same-sex sexual behavior is to not purposely throw themselves into the midst of gay culture.

This was by far my biggest stumbling block at the beginning. Looking back I feel as though I lost a lot of potentially productive time in the GLBT community. Every gay or lesbian person I came in contact with, especially when it came to my best friends, I couldn't help but picture them naked—having sex with someone of the same sex. I wasted so much time thinking of sex that I had no chance to concentrate on listening, learning and building a bridge.

Second, Christians should do their homework beforehand. A great friend of The Marin Foundation and a former seminary professor of mine, Dr. John Fuder, teaches the importance of exegeting the culture. We have to go to the culture before we know the culture. For most of us this comes in slowly taken smaller steps toward involvement. The key is to not overwhelm ourselves into hating our attempts to build sustainable relationships with GLBT people. It's important to know limits. If something turns out to be too much, realize it's too much and back away until you're ready again for another go around. Whether it is walking around your local gay neighborhood and silently praying for a learning, nonconfrontational spirit, attending a local chapter of a larger gay organization and just sitting silently in the back of the room listening, or asking a GLBT person to go get coffee and talk about everything but GLBT-Christian issues, a step in the right direction is always one step in. Step-by-step involvement over time is not a failure; it's intelligently approaching productive bridge building.

A seventy-nine-year-old Christian woman named Pamela used to be a nurse in a large city before her retirement. When AIDS started rapidly spreading in the 1980s she saw her share of gay men quickly die on her watch. Those images never left her memory, and a few years ago she felt God was calling her to once again get involved with the GLBT community. Pamela, who also has a heart for the elderly, realized that there were probably elderly GLBT people who needed to be cared for. Her thoughts were right. Many elderly GLBT people have lost friends and loved ones not only to advanced age but also prematurely in years past to HIV. After a few phone calls and some research on the Internet, sure enough there was a group offering that exact service. For the last two years Pamela has been volunteering at a GLBT hospice, where elderly gay men and women who can't care for themselves receive the care they need.

A friend who has HIV said to me, "What brings on spirituality more than mortality?" Pamela has found that to be true, and uses her longing to serve as an opportunity to show God's love to elderly GLBT people.

Third, we have to prepare ourselves to not say or do anything that would be contrary to our intent to learn or serve—to not preach at, argue with, fight or debate gays and lesbians on their territory. Their space is not our space, and as Christians enter into their world we must remember to be thankful for such unique learning opportunities. It is fine to have someone accompany you if the thought of getting involved alone is too overwhelming. I have many Christians tell me that they feel as though they have a heart for gays and lesbians, but are too afraid to even attempt to do anything about it. Preparatory prayer and a humbled mindset of learning and serving release much of the fear of trying to single-handedly pave a path to make new culture.

NOTICING MATTERS

The last simple way Christians can step toward the GLBT community is to seek out those who don't fit in. Be intentional about talking to someone who might not look like everyone else, might not fit in with the in crowd or might be a loner. Some loners choose to be that way, but many feel as though they have been given no other option.

Think about the two emails earlier in the chapter. What if someone in either one of their lives had shown interest in what was truly happening on the inside? Would their worldview of faith, Christianity and God have turned out any differently? There is no telling, because no one can take back past experiences. At the very least though, neither of them would have felt like some type of segregated, cast-out freak show within the confines of a belief system and surrounding group of like-minded people who should be able to provide a sense of home, comfort and trust.

Shame and stigma are difficult to quantify because they are ultimately internal feelings. By giving attention to the GLBT community's social, political and religious experiences in mainstream society as well as within the church, Christians have a magnificent opportunity to dynamically cultivate relationships through shared experiences with a traditionally ostracized GLBT culture.

4

Gay Versus Christian
and Gay Christians

Turn on the television at any given point throughout the day and there's a good chance you'll see warring entities slinging personal theology from one side to the other. In that setting the winner always emerges as the one who can speak more quickly and loudly and dominate the conversation. After his appearance on MSNBC, a Christian media figure emailed me and told me how he "manhandled" the other guest, whom I also know because he works for a GLBT organization The Marin Foundation has been involved with.

The way that the argumentative nature of the strained conservative-GLBT relationship has been publicized does more harm to both communities than it ever will do for good. But constructive dialogue just doesn't make good TV now, does it? This "war" has been paraded around like a circus and because of that, dissension and violent opposition have become the norm that each community feels is the proper way to handle the other. I can safely say that Scripture was never meant to be used to try to beleaguer and embarrass others on national TV, or for that matter, to draw unnecessary attention to yourself.

Unfortunately none of those tactics will be easily changed because the deeply permeated ethos to the fighting cannot be escaped: the interpretation of Scripture—defined as the all-inclusive word of

God that blesses same-sex relationships—no, I mean the judgmental Father who casts off gays and lesbians to their rightful place in hell—um, I'm actually talking about the Scripture that is only culturally relevant to its historical context and is not talking about monogamous same-sex relationships—well, it's really the Scripture that accounts for behavioral choices regardless of orientation—or maybe it's the . . .

You get the point. Evangelicals believe (as do I) that the Bible is the inerrant word of God, God-breathed by the Holy Spirit through human authorship. When I started The Marin Foundation I was twenty-four years old and had been immersed in the GLBT community for almost six years. But in those six years my experience had been purely relational—mostly through one-on-one interactions with my best friends, people I met at gay bars and clubs, and people who attended the Bible study group. I thought I had seen and experienced enough within those six years that nothing could shock me. It was not until I officially represented The Marin Foundation that I began to see firsthand how systemic and theological differences, as well as a blatant felt-hatred, were played out on a regular basis between the two communities. When I started getting involved with gay churches, gay Christians, and Christian churches and straight Christians who hated gay churches and gay Christians, and vice versa, I quickly realized that the word *Christian* was just a word—nothing more.

It was a bad label that communicated scorn and ridicule between the two communities who were each trying to prove that their version of *Christian* was the correct version. "My Christian is better than your Christian. You're not a Christian. The Jesus I know wouldn't do those things or say any of that!" *Christian* was no longer a belief; it wasn't a religion, and it sure wasn't what God intended it to be or what Jesus made it.

Alas, I was convinced that each day I woke up I was to be pushed, battered and thrown into a complete mess that totally tested everything I faithfully believed and thought to be true. The battlefield had been marked, the teams were assembled, and I was tired of trying to be persuaded to join one side or the other when I didn't believe in what either was doing. My heart yearned for authentic Christianity—one where people from both communities lived together in a shared belief in Christ amidst the stuggle.

THE WORDS I NEVER THOUGHT I'D HEAR FROM A PASTOR

During a typical hot and muggy Chicago summer day I was in the office of a gay pastor in one of Chicago's more upscale neighborhoods talking about the bridge-building vision of The Marin Foundation. Although I know this pastor does not speak for all gay pastors, he interrupted me and flat-out told me that he intentionally disregards entire sections of the Bible because he believes that they are not correct, not inspired and do nothing but harm the GLBT community. He then quickly asked me what I thought about that. As I was about to answer the question, he not so subtly crossed his legs, folded his arms and sat back in his chair with a smug look on his face. Looking at him, my only thought was that he must have felt pretty proud of himself trying to trap me, just waiting for me to say something I probably would regret.

Over the years I have met people in the GLBT community who say things like that to get the Christian's blood going, but I had never heard it come from a professing pastor. I guess this was my baptism by fire. I knew someday, someone was bound to say it, but I never realized how much it would actually affect me.

I sat kind of awkwardly with a puzzled look on my face, trying to get over the shock that those words came out of a shepherd's mouth. I kept thinking to myself, *how can someone who loves the Word so dearly not be totally offended by that statement?* With a half-smile on my face I asked him to expand so I could figure out what he really meant. We ended up having an interesting conversation—well, it actually just consisted of him lecturing me in a harsh voice and giving me Pro-Gay Theology 101 for about an hour before he said he had another meeting and promptly asked me to leave his office.

THE WORDS I NEVER THOUGHT I'D HEAR FROM GOD

As I left I began to pray to God that not every gay pastor, or gay Christian for that matter, would be like that pastor. If that was going to be the case I knew The Marin Foundation was finished before it ever really got started. I realized that I couldn't handle or react to such antagonistic behavior with any civility. How was I to ever build a bridge when I loathed the person sitting across from me as he intentionally tried to rile me up and cause an argument?

Standing at a familiar bus stop across from that gay church, I devised a plan to ensure that I would always get the last word. With my chest puffed up, I suddenly heard God say, "What if every professing gay pastor or gay Christian you ever meet for the rest of your life is exactly like that pastor? Does that make what I have asked you to do any less relevant? Now go and do as I have commanded."

I had never been humiliated and humbled so quickly. With my tail between my legs and an apology to God in tow, Joshua 1:9 came to mind: "Have I not commanded you? Be strong and courageous. Do not be terrified; do not be discouraged, for the LORD your God will be with you wherever you go."

And there it was. He and his words and his goals for my life, for the GLBT community and for his kingdom supersede any encounter I might not ever want to have again. There is a bigger plan at work, and it's sure bigger than any potentially negative experiences that might come forth—and for a brief second in my self-pity and anger toward that gay pastor I forgot all of that.

This sobering message refocused my thoughts and set my mind on a new path. From that point on, each day for the next six months I set up meetings with every gay pastor and gay church I could find in the city of Chicago. I would get together with them—two, three, four of them per day—to learn about their beliefs and figure out how to somehow get involved.

Even at this early stage I knew I didn't want to wake up one day and be "that guy" yelling on TV, constantly trying to manhandle the opposition. I knew what I believed as truth, and for the first time I realized that the security in what I believed was not contingent upon other people having to agree with me. If I could only understand the ins and outs of what gay Christians believed I could begin to understand how to best represent Jesus within the GLBT community.

THE SPECTRUM OF GAY AND CHRISTIAN

What about your life though? Many of you are not going to have that same experience. In fact, I know many people who go out of their way to avoid any such situation. Living in the midst of both worlds, I have seen how Christians too easily resort to traditional stereotypes about gay Christians—rather than building off of a common ground in Christ and seeing each of them for who they are. Gay Christians are a compilation of individual journeys and lives that have been filled with unique experiences that we can never have.

One of the most common scenarios that happens, more than any of us might be willing to admit, is that conservative churches employ gay Christians not knowing they're gay. In fact, a very well-known church in the Midwest employs three gay Christians in key positions and they don't even know! Those three people regularly talk to me because they don't know where else to turn. I find that to be quite the unfortunate oxymoron—these three people all work at a church and they *still* don't have anywhere to turn.

Most gay Christians live in so much fear that they have learned how to proficiently blend in to their conservative surroundings. It's a great chameleon job on their part, but it's a heartbreakingly lost opportunity for authenticity on ours.

Almost two years ago I met a man named Tim. He was, and still is, working at a large evangelical church in Chicago, and until he told me his story I could have never discerned his past. Five years ago a pastor who understood who Christ really is rallied his church community to make a new life for Tim. Last year Tim was asked to give his testimony at all three of his church's services. Beforehand he and I talked about how he was going to relate his life experiences without turning off anyone in attendance, gay or straight. He knows what it's like to be stuck in between, and because of the prominence of his church in their community, many onlookers from all walks of life would be in attendance judging each word. But when the time came for Tim to get on the stage he scrapped most of what we talked about and let it fly from his heart. Tim opened his time by boldly saying, "The opposite of homosexuality is not heterosexuality. It's wholeness."

This is a concept I had never heard before—profound and very controversial in many evangelical circles, including the one he was speaking to. I sat there looking around at the congregation to gauge their reactions to such a statement.

People were absorbing each of Tim's words from that moment on.

Silence kills—secrets aren't kept forever. There are some things you can say and there are other things you can't, especially inside the church. You can mention pornography, masturbation, drug addiction and everything in between and find some sort of hope of forgiveness and acceptance from the church (not acceptance as if it's OK, but acceptance that there is hope). *But*—and it's a big but—there's one word that turns people red in the face and shuts their mouths. I'm talking about being gay. By the time I was seven, I had heard fag, homo and sissy spoken my direction too often. I was always very active at church, and in my heart I thought the more I do the more likely this will go away.

It didn't; it just got worse. In a place where you think you could talk to someone and be real with what was going on, the only feeling I got when I'd even think that I could muster up the courage to talk about my life was one of fear. What would people say? How would they react? I wished that I could have struggled with looking at *Playboy*. At least then I would be somewhat normal. How, as a kid in high school, do you go to your youth pastor and tell him you are attracted to people of the same sex when he does such a great "gay" impersonation that everyone seems to think is hilarious?

You don't. So I just kept quiet. I never said a word as I thought at some point it would pass. I tried everything I knew—fasted, prayed, read the Bible. I was so desperate.

A few years passed and I was on staff at a church across the country from where I grew up. The night before I was about to fly home and visit my parents, I got "outed." I was great at covering up, but the Internet history told a wild tale. For the first time in fifteen years, in the company of people whom I loved and trusted, I talked about the abuse that happened when I was younger and about my struggle with silence. I bore my soul and all of the pain that came with that silence. As difficult as that moment was, it was a moment that I had longed for. I felt freedom for the first time. But instead of finding hope, I was told to box up everything I had and then leave! They ended up dropping me off, alone, for three days in a $29.99-per-night motel on the south side of town that was surrounded by barbed wire, with only $15 to my name. I found out after I returned home that the lead pastor at that church had called everyone he knew from my hometown and told them everything that happened, attempting to bar me from any type of normalcy.

When I finally got home and saw everyone at my old church I fully expected to get the same response. Instead the senior pastor took my hands in his and looked me in the eyes and said, "Tim, I believe in you. I believe you are called by God and I know God has a special plan for your life. What they did to you was wrong, and I'm sorry . . . and know that I love you, want to help you and can't think of a better place for you to be than on staff at this church."

It was so amazing for me to see in the span of one week how the church can respond to the issue of homosexuality. On one end, I was discarded, told I was broken and was left alone. And on the other I was loved, embraced and set on a path that brought great healing to my life.

Change is a word that is often emotionally associated with this topic. God brought wholeness into my life and I began to see myself as God saw me. My identity wasn't rooted in my past, but in Christ. I don't believe change is the absence of struggle, but it's having the freedom to choose in the midst of the struggle what I know to be God's intended path for my life.

I want to get married and have a family but I don't believe that being married and having a family will be an end to my struggle or sign that I'm "healed." My sin is no different than yours, and God's grace is here to meet us all at our point of need. I am here not as someone who used to be gay, but as one of you. I am an undeserving sinner who has encountered God's amazing grace.

Do you think Tim is right in his own assessment of his life? What if Tim didn't want to get married and instead remained celibate? Would he be a gay Christian in your eyes—because I know many people in Tim's exact situation who still call themselves gay Christians. What about men and women who are actively involved in the GLBT community and profess to be Christians? Are they gay Christians as well? If they are, are they the same gay Christian that Tim calls himself? Does he still identify with them—is that even OK? These are all questions for Tim, not for those of us who do not feel same-sex attractions. Christians should not be answering these questions *for* them, but living life *with* those who have them.

This next section will piece together the pro-gay theological hermeneutic. Take it for what it's worth. Read it. Soak it in. I am not asking you to agree with their beliefs, but I am asking you to humbly learn their views from their perspective. I will not be arguing and attempting to prove this belief system wrong, but rather putting it out there as a key component to understanding the GLBT mindset.

It is as important to understand pro-gay theology as it is to understand the gay filtration system on Christian apologetics. The Gay Apologetic breaks down into seven sections: general beliefs; general biblical thoughts; an Old Testament gay apologetic; a New Testament gay apologetic; a social apologetic; an intertwined social and biblical apologetic; and eight premises, developed by gay Christian leader Mel White (www.soulforce.org), on what the Bible says and doesn't say about homosexuality.

GAY CHRISTIAN GENERAL BELIEFS

First, the GLBT community sees objections to homosexuality by evangelical Christians as a form of unjust religious bigotry. The GLBT community has battled their way to what they know of religious freedom. If Christians are not willing to recognize that, they're doing nothing more than causing unrighteous oppression.

Mel White, a now openly gay man who during his closeted years was a speechwriter and ghostwriter for Billy Graham, Pat Robertson, Jim Bakker and Jerry Falwell, succinctly sums up the broader gay Christian thought: "Like you, I take the Bible seriously." Gay Christians want to be taken seriously just like heterosexual Christians. The best way to take gay Christians seriously is to presume that the Word of God is being taken in truthful reverence.

GAY CHRISTIAN GENERAL BIBLICAL THOUGHTS

Gay Christians believe that the passages in the Bible that condemn same-sex relationships are not referencing long-term, committed monogamous relationships. Rather, the Bible is talking about inhospitality, heterosexual rape, pagan ritual sex and orgies, and pederasty (men having sex with boys).

They also believe that translations and interpretations of the Bible are unclear relative to the hermeneutical historical-cultural/transcultural analysis of homosexuality. Since the Bible does not discuss long-term, committed monogamous same-sex relationships, what was applicable for the Israelites and early Christians in their specific historical period is not applicable for gay Christians today.

The key factors that glue the Bible's overarching principles together throughout both Testaments are the call to love our neighbor and have compassion on the oppressed, and that God gives each of us an ability to receive freedom in Christ. Among many other verses, gay Christians refer to Jesus' words about the greatest commandment in Matthew 22:37-40 and Mark 12:29-31.

OLD TESTAMENT GAY APOLOGETIC

The Sodom and Gomorrah story (Gen 19) is not talking about longterm, committed monogamous same-sex relationships—it is talking about gay rape, which violates the hospitality laws of the day (Ezek 16:49). The parallel passage to Sodom and Gomorrah is the story in Judges 19:22-26, which consists of heterosexual rape, again highlighting the main theme of rape in concordance with Genesis 19.

Same-sex sexual relations are one of many issues addressed in the Holiness Code (Leviticus), which also prohibits such things as wearing clothing woven of two kinds of material, getting tattoos, planting two kinds of seed together, playing with the skin of a pig and mating different kinds of animals together. Offenders are burned by the fire, executed, stoned to death or kicked out of the community. All told, 613 laws—including the sanctions regarding same-sex sexual relations—are connected by the Holiness Code to salvation, which Jesus' redemptive blood washed over in the New Covenant, and therefore they are not to be generalized for today.

Also, same-sex relationships in the Bible, such as Jonathan and David (1-2 Samuel) and Ruth and Naomi (Ruth), are thought by a small percentage of gay Christians to be physically sexual relationships.

NEW TESTAMENT GAY APOLOGETIC

Jesus was silent on the issue of homosexuality. Which begs the question: if homosexuality is so important, why did Jesus not say one word about it?

A Roman centurion asked Jesus to heal his servant (Mt 8:5-13; Lk

7:1-10). The Greek word for servant is *pais*, which can literally mean a male lover. *Pais*, sexual servants, were very common in the ancient Near East Roman culture, and Jesus would have known this. Therefore Jesus was not opposed to homosexuality.

According to ancient literature, eunuchs could be manmade (castrated) or naturally born (incapable of—or disinterested in—intercourse with women). As one gay Christian author puts it, "To introduce one's self as a eunuch in ancient times was roughly akin to introducing one's self today as a hairdresser from San Francisco."[1] Therefore Philip's baptism of a eunuch (Acts 8:26-40) confirmed that gay men are accepted in the kingdom.

Paul's condemnation of same-sex sexual relations in Romans 1:26-27 as "unnatural" is once again not referring to long-term, committed monogamous relationships. He is specifically talking about the common Roman practice of pederasty, in which older males "mentor," or have sex with, male children, which is legitimately denounced as unnatural and caused by a depraved mind.

Gay apologists believe that Paul coined the word *arsenokoitēs* (1 Cor 6:9-11) as he was referring to older males who were customers of male "call boys" or prostitutes. This practice was common during the Greco-Roman period. It wasn't until 1946 in the Revised Standard Version (RSV) that a Bible translator decided to label the unknown *arsenokoitēs* as "homosexual offender." A similar debate persists with 1 Timothy 1:10.

GAY SOCIAL APOLOGETIC

Homosexuality is an orientation, not a lifestyle. This topic will be discussed in more depth in chapter ten.

Homosexuality is genetic: although there has been a historic push over the last decade to complete a research study that infallibly shows a link from homosexuality to a specific gene(s), none have been able to be successfully duplicated to validate that claim. Currently in many circles both gay and straight, scientific and religious, there has been a more common acceptance of homosexuality's etiology as a combination of biological, environmental and social factors that all contribute to gay orientation.

The APA does not list homosexuality in the *Diagnostic and Statistical Manual of Mental Disorders (DSM—IV):* if the American Psychological Association (APA) believes homosexuality is not a defect, disease or disorder, it should then be recognized as religiously acceptable—as opposed to being a behavior that needs to be modified.

There is an ever-increasing number of the population coming out as gay, lesbian, bisexual and transgender: Christendom has oppressed the GLBT community for so long that many people over the decades were too terrified to come out and show the world who they really are. Since gay apologetics are becoming more well known within religious circles, as well as within mainstream culture, more GLBT people will continue to show their faces until the Christian community recognizes that GLBT people have also been created by the Creator. There are too many GLBT people for them to be a mistake by God.

INTERTWINED BIBLICAL AND
SOCIAL GAY APOLOGETIC

Gay Christians believe the Bible is used to justify homophobia, judgmentalism and segregation. This improper use of Scripture directly leads to the cultural stigma and shame GLBT people feel within the mainstream.

GLBT orientation can't be changed and therefore it is God's way of telling GLBT people it's a happy, healthy and God-ordained way of life; otherwise he wouldn't have created GLBT people as such. Equality rights and legalized same-sex marriage are a byproduct of this thought.

If homosexuality is wrong, how can a GLBT person be a born-again believer and filled with the Spirit, able to use those gifts to bless the kingdom and positively influence nonbelievers' spiritual lives? Gay Christians have started to change the mainstream's mindset that GLBT people crave random sex, are STD-laced, and have alcohol and drug problems.

MEL WHITE'S 8 PREMISES

By all accounts Dr. Mel White has been the most prominent and vocal leader of the rising gay Christian movement. His eight premises, outlined in a booklet titled *What the Bible Says—and Doesn't Say —About Homosexuality,* have been used as the basis for the ever-growing understanding of what Christians know today as a pro-gay theology. These eight premises are Dr. White's biblical responses to the question "How can you consider yourself a Christian when you are also gay?"

1. Most people have not carefully and prayerfully researched the biblical texts often used to condemn GLBT children.

2. Historically, people's misinterpretation of the Bible has left a trail of suffering, bloodshed and death.

3. Christians must be open to new truth from Scripture. Even heroes of the Christian faith have changed their minds about the meaning of various biblical texts.

4. The Bible is a book about God—not about human sexuality: It condemns sexual practices we accept and we accept sexual practices it condemns.

5. We miss what the passages say about God when we spend so much time debating what it says about sex.

6. The biblical authors are silent about GLBT orientation as we know it today. They neither approve it or condemn it.

7. Although the prophets, Jesus and other biblical authors say nothing about GLBT orientation as we understand it today, they are clear about one thing: As we search for truth, we are to "love one another."

8. Whatever some people believe the Bible says about homosexuality, they must not use that belief to deny the GLBT community their basic civil rights. To discriminate against sexual or gender minorities is unjust and un-American.

Although this is far from an exhaustive look into gay apologetics, these are the key points that many gay Christians believe. In order to elevate the conversation about the Christian faith and the GLBT community, we need to seek out conversation partners and talk through these key points knowing that both partners will be committed without knowing where the conversations will ultimately lead them.

WHAT CAN CHRISTIANS DO?

Find a gay church with a gay pastor; ask to get together with them so you can listen and learn. The best approach to doing this is to open with something like the following: "Can you please tell me what you believe the Bible says about same-sex sexual attraction and how you arrived at your conclusions? I don't want to fight. I don't want to argue. I just want to learn from you about something I know little about from your perspective."

I have had many seminary students, pastors and everyday Christians over the years tell me that they would love to learn more about the GLBT community and their theological beliefs, but they are afraid that they'll say the wrong thing and ultimately do more harm than good. But there is no wrong way to humbly listen and learn!

Next, invite GLBT people to your church. This morning alone I had eight new voicemails, and five of them were from GLBT people I don't know—some gay Christians, some nonreligious and some just wanting spiritual help. All called from 6 p.m. the previous evening to 8 a.m. this morning. That overnight amount of GLBT calling is not an aberration. The GLBT community is interested in the things of God. If we're not going to help them search for what they're looking for, which is ultimately the same thing we're looking for, then they'll do it themselves without our help.

Have you ever sung a praise and worship song next to a gay Christian before? I don't know how you would feel, but I'll never forget the first time I did. I stood there looking to my right and my left at the people I had invited and I was completely puzzled. They sang the same songs as I did. They raised their hands just like me.

They closed their eyes and sang from the depths of their soul as I have done my entire life. I don't know what I expected to happen, but I sure didn't expect that.

The entire time I couldn't concentrate on the songs, the worship or even the sermon. I was just trying to search in my spirit what the Lord thought about all of this. I was planning to take that pending revelation and shout it from the mountaintops. What did I hear? What did I get from the Lord that Sunday? Absolutely nothing. How annoying is that!

I realized through the nothingness that this experience—this time of worship—was only supposed to be about him. It was not about acceptance, validation or condemnation of gays and lesbians. It was not about the gay Christian movement, a pro-gay theology or traditional biblical interpretations of Scripture. It was not about differences or similarities or anything that my mind could futilely try to comprehend that morning. It was about Jesus. It's always been about Jesus and I lost sight of that.

For the very first time I substantially knew in the depths of my soul that I didn't have to worry about all of those other things because they were not mine to worry about. I was making it my deal, making it my baggage and making it my worry, and I didn't have to do any of that. When did I become God? When did I have to figure it all out? When did I have to come up with a position point on every single topic ever thought of in the history of mankind? I didn't; and I don't. I am allowed the ability to just trust in the faithfulness of my loving Father to fill in the gaps that I can never understand.

The freedom that came with my simplistic revelation that God is God took the weight of the whole GLBT religious world off of my heavily burdened, weak shoulders. Let the all-knowing God be God, and you be you.

GLBT people coming to church should be a celebration, instead of the head-turning fright festival it quickly turns into. One Christian ex-gay author reflects the broader Christian mindset when he contends that the church has no choice but to fight with the gay community. Coexistence, he suggests, is a practical impossibility.[2] We've spent too much time destroying possibilities of hope for the GLBT community. It needs to change.

Christians have been trained to think that one attempt at relational redemption will then take away a GLBT person's pain and hurt. It just doesn't work like that. People just don't forgive and forget that quickly. Sometimes I actually believe that Christians dig themselves a bigger hole on purpose just so there is a built-in excuse to point the finger and say, "See, they don't want to build a bridge. I just reached out." If the body of Christ is to truly make a difference you must first drop the overt argument mindset. I don't care what either side says, this is not a war. This is not a battle. There are no soldiers and there is no governmental talking head, no matter how much both sides try to bring the issue before the courts. Until the body of Christ believes that peaceful productivity with gays and lesbians is actually an option, how can we ever expect it to happen?

This is the first main step to how Christians begin to elevate the conversation past a street fight. It's a lot like the first step God commanded Joshua to take into the flooded Jordan River before the Israelites could cross into the Promised Land (Josh 3). Take a small, yet difficult and uncertain step with the Lord toward another person—even with a very real feeling of overwhelming trepidation for what might happen—and just watch what happens as that little step inaugurates life-altering redemptive conversations about the things of God with the GLBT community.

5

Who Are We Looking to
for Validation?

The GLBT Quest for Good News from God

Imagine you're in the clouds looking down on the Golden Gate
Bridge. It's suspended above the Golden Gate Strait, connecting
the San Francisco Bay to the Pacific Ocean, and you can see that
the bridge is anchored down by two large landmasses on each
side. On one side is the gay and lesbian community firmly bolted
down. On the other is the evangelical community firmly planted
in the same fashion.

Now from your position in the clouds, remove the entire middle
section of the Golden Gate Bridge. What's left are two brief entrance
ramps still anchored on each side with nothing to connect them.
Imagine the GLBT community and the Christian community standing on their respective sides, sincerely and honestly encouraging
one another to leave their safe and secure landmass and swim
across to the other side, pull themselves out of the water, try to
climb up the entrance ramp without ropes or any equipment, and
then somehow stumble their way to the other community who is
comfortably waiting, wondering what took so long.

There's got to be a better way.

CONSTRUCTING THE BRIDGE BRINGS
A HARSH REALITY

Christians' first move has to come unapologetically in love and humility by building a solid foundation of what we know to be true not only in our faith but also within the gay and lesbian community. We need to start giving of ourselves more than we receive in return. We need to start letting our guard down more than our fears will ever allow. Reconciliation can only begin by searching our own souls and unabashedly uncovering our own secret conceits and prejudices.

When the Golden Gate Bridge was being constructed there was a group of men who literally risked their lives by working to build the middle section of the suspension bridge—they called themselves the "halfway to hell club." By no means am I associating building a bridge with the GLBT community as being halfway to hell, but in the same fashion as those workers, we have to realize the risk we're taking by choosing to work from the middle. When you make a cognizant decision to step out for God's bridge-building work and expose your soul, you will be lashed out against as well as quickly confronted with and harshly ushered into a world of someone else's long-lasting pain. Everything you have tried to work your way around biblically, socially and culturally will be brought to your doorstep, demanding an answer. This is a lot of pressure; in fact it is too much pressure for us to carry ourselves. Therefore these next chapters will ask the key questions to open and unlock the minds of the evangelical community—learning how to tangibly build that bridge with gays and lesbians.

BEGINNING TO ELEVATE THE CONVERSATION

How can Christians even think of building a bridge when theologically *and* socially, these two communities don't agree on much of anything? I believe that there are five biblical principles which elevate the conversation with gays and lesbians. I call them the Big 5, and each of them is hermeneutically based out of the verses in the

Bible that speak directly to the topic of homosexuality. The Big 5 will be expanded on further in chapters seven and eight, but the concept of elevating the conversation needs to be introduced at this juncture.

One cannot work within the GLBT community without facing the tough questions that are on the tip of everyone's mind—is homosexuality right or wrong; nature or nurture; sin or non-sin; "out and proud" or ex-gay? The purpose of elevating the conversation is not to answer those questions for you, but rather to give you the framework for gays and lesbians to answer those questions with you by their side.

Ever since I first immersed myself, no matter where I go to hang out, speak, train, educate, listen or learn I have been asked those same questions by both sides over and over again. Without a doubt they are always the first things I'm asked, and I've learned how to handle such divisive questions without causing a further divide. To elevate the conversation is to change the conversation—moving the starting point of the conversation to the starting point of the conversation partner.

Eric Leocadio, a well-known gay blogger from Long Beach, California (twoworldcollision.blogspot.com), has a poignant take on the elevation approach to building a bridge between evangelicals and gays and lesbians.

> Since [Andrew Marin] is a straight man, many people are concerned about what it is that he's about. Some gay people are concerned that he's advocating for "change." Some straight conservative people are concerned that he's advocating for the "gay lifestyle." Some are concerned that he's either, both or neither. I can see why some would find him hard to read because he approaches the "issue" differently than most. He doesn't make it a gay or straight issue. He . . . talks about more important things—spiritual growth while trusting Jesus to communicate to an individual his heart and will through a growing relationship with him. [As I try working] with others

from various organizations who want to navigate the "hot zone" [the gay/religious issue] . . . I think the key for all of us is to start teaching this new language to both sides of the bridge so that we can one day begin to talk with each other.

Eric realizes that too much structural damage has been done on both sides for some quick patchwork. This debate, or the "hot zone" as he calls it, needs a total resurfacing.

If I have only learned one thing through all my years immersed in the GLBT community it's that gays and lesbians can read. I know— quite a discovery. I jokingly say that with a serious undertow—many gays and lesbians can quote the Bible better than a majority of Christians I know. Why? Because they feel they've been beaten down by the Bible for so long that their only defense is to know it better than those attacking them. The unfortunate repercussion is that the Bible has become a defensive literary tool rather than a powerful book written by Jehovah. What is eventually discovered is that no matter how strong of a literary knowledge base someone might have, if it's not in the context of spiritual growth with God the intellectual understanding fades into a shallow and insufficient mode of defense.

WHERE DOES ETERNAL VALIDATION COME FROM?

The GLBT community has tended to look to others for legitimacy regarding who they are and what sexual behaviors they have— whether that validation comes from other gays and lesbians, from sections of the religious community or from mainstream culture. I believe this widespread search for validity is the primary reason that so many GLBT faith and religion organizations exist today. I also believe this is why they fight so fiercely against evangelicals— they are longing to be validated by the one group that has yet to offer it.

But when all is said and done only God can truly validate and judge anyone or anything. From my vantage point the GLBT community has been searching within the wrong sources. A gay pastor's

validation can't get someone into heaven. A gay politician's validation can't get someone into heaven. A gay biologist's validation can't
get someone into heaven. A gay lawyer's validation can't get someone into heaven. A gay scientist's validation can't get someone into
heaven. A gay psychologist's validation can't get someone into
heaven. A gay anything's validation can't get anyone into heaven.
And don't you dare forget—a straight anything's validation or judgments won't be able to send anyone to heaven or hell either! Only
God can.

With a refocused shift onto God, the only way to get close enough
to hear this validation or rebuke is by having an intimate, personal
relationship. This might not be a new conclusion, but it is when it
comes to the GLBT community. Christians look at a gay or lesbian
person and see a potential behavioral change instead of a person
longing to know the same Christ we seek. If we could only release
control of what might happen down the road in a GLBT person's life
when Jesus enters, I promise that God loves his children enough to
always tell each of them what he feels is best for their life.

So then why not start peacefully pointing gays and lesbians in
the direction of learning how to have an intimate, real, conversational relationship with the Father and Judge instead of trying to
put all of them in 12-step programs? Like all other groups, including straight believers, GLBT people are nothing more than sheep
looking for their shepherd.

In pointing gays and lesbians to God it is ultimately that person's
choice to either accept, decline or just sit on it until they're good
and ready to do something. Christians need to take a lesson from
the field of clinical psychology. One of the first things therapists are
taught is to get comfortable with silence. Why? Because if the psychologist is not comfortable with the silence then they prematurely
blurt out unnecessary comments just to fill the awkward silent
space. In the process they break what is often a productive tension.

Just the same, Christians also need to understand that the word
no is a legitimate response to any offer, no matter how life-changing

we might think that offer is. The Christian-GLBT relationship is contentious at best, and no relationship can be secure when it is constantly under the threat of a barrage of apologetics. The Christian wet blanket of suffocation that demands timely answers or spontaneous thoughts to accept or deny Jesus or some other Christian truth, without allowing the productive tension of just "being" with that idea in support and love, doesn't build bridges: it ruins kingdom opportunities.

ETERNAL VALIDATION IS NOT FROM HUMANS

Don't think that the GLBT community has been the only one searching for validation in the wrong arenas. For years Christians have also sought out external earthly means to validate their claims against GLBT people. This has landed the Christian community in an intense, tireless search for supporting evidence in social, psychological, biological, sociological, anthropological and biblical fields to validate their traditional interpretation of Scripture as correct. No matter who comes up with whatever rationale, or how many gays and lesbians turn to God, nothing can eternally validate Christians' truth claims anyway. Only God can do that.

Yet the forum of a debate, not God, has become the only acceptable medium to figure out whose evidence is more legitimate. If God is the only one who can actually validate or judge anyone or anything, then why are we fighting so hard to prove a point that has already been made? Conservative pastors, conservative politicians, conservative lawyers, conservative biologists, conservative psychologists—none of these can make us right with God or one another. I promise that God loves his children enough that he will always tell each of them what he feels is best for their life. I believe that Christians are held more responsible because we have had the unchanging Word of God to learn from the mistakes of those who came before.

God reprimanded the Israelites in the Old Testament for seeking earthly validation by conforming to the ways of the world—insisting on a human king to rule over them. Samuel petitioned God on behalf of the Israelites and the Lord said,

> It is not you they have rejected, but they have rejected me as their king. As they have done from the day I brought them up out of Egypt until this day, forsaking me and serving other gods, so they are doing to you. Now listen to them; but warn them solemnly and let them know what the king who will reign over them will do.

Even after Samuel told the Israelites the horrors of what was to come with a human king they repeated, "We want a king over us. Then we will be like all the other nations, with a king to lead us and to go out before us and fight our battles" (1 Sam 8:6-20).

Just the same, in the New Testament God reprimanded the early church through Paul, who shamed the Corinthians for going to the outside pagan legal system for their validation regarding internal matters that even the least of Christians should be more competent in justice to handle than the wisest of pagans (1 Cor 6:1-6).[1] Christians are to look within our own belief system in how to live our lives righteously.

Validation comes from the Father alone, discerned through each individual as it pertains to their relationship with him, not from any other earthly being, organization, celebrity, dogmatic expression or perceived religious duty to another. He will always answer, and he will always do what is good in his sight for those who earnestly seek his voice (2 Sam 10:12).

The way forward with the GLBT community is not a debate on the Bible's statements about same-sex sexual behavior but a discussion of how to have an intimate, real, conversational relationship with the Father and Judge.

THE TROUBLE WITH NORMAL

Michael Warner, a gay professor of English at Yale University, wrote the book *The Trouble with Normal* as a critique of secularism, ethics, sexual shame, politics and gay marriage from a nontraditional gay perspective. In it he challenges the GLBT community to look at various social constructs differently.

Warner believes that same-sex marriage should not be legalized because it plays into the conservative Christian belief that marriage is the ultimate expression of love. For him, same-sex marriage is a means of conformity to Christianity. He states, "Those of us who have already fought our way to an identity and a supportive environment may feel that we no longer need that material evidence."[2] If gay and lesbian couples were the ones who fought the hard fight against shame, cultural stigma and religious ostracization—without the support of Christianity—and still somehow found their way to a personally acceptable gay identity surrounded by loving friends and "a supportive environment," why would they ever need the "material evidence" of a Christian institution such as marriage?

I am challenged by Warner's thoughts as he pushes the cultural bounds of what it means to live a life void of religious validation—and yet he, as a gay man, is able to make a compelling argument against same-sex marriage. Warner succinctly elevated the conversation from a secularist point of view, and in terms of same-sex marriage there is also a way to elevate the conversation from a bridge-building point of view. Imagine with me that one of two options happen with same-sex marriage: (a) it is uniformly legalized throughout the country, or (b) a bill is passed that completely bans same-sex marriage—and that bill also states that it can never again be brought up for a vote for the remainder of people's existence on earth. Which one would you want to see happen?

From an elevated perspective neither option matters. Christian parents all over the country are already forced to have difficult conversations with their children about why their kid's friends have two moms or two dads living in the same "marriage" capacity as the Christian parents—regardless if those two moms or two dads are legally married or not.

In research done by The Williams Institute and the Urban Institute, more than 65,000 adopted children are living with gay or lesbian parents in the United States. The same research also showed that over 14,000 foster children (3 percent of all foster children) are living with gay or lesbian foster parents. Preventing legalized same-sex marriage, or legalizing it, is not going to change those difficult conversations for any Christian family. In this case Christians are once again working off of a false model of the ideal situation.

As Shane Claiborne and Chris Haw acknowledge in their book *Jesus for President,* we find ourselves in a fallen world that dominates government and culture in ways that are not of our Father. It is not the Christian community's responsibility to govern a world that we do not belong to; fight in wars that are in direct opposition to Jesus' peaceful, nonviolent approach; or reign over a government we are not a part of.

> For Jesus and his followers, the central question was, How do we live faithfully to God? . . . [The central question was not,] How do we run the world as Christians? . . . How do I run this profit-driven corporation as a Christian? . . . How can we make culture more Christian? How would a responsible Christian run this war? But Jesus taught that his followers—or even the Son of God!—should not attempt to "run the world."[3]

Let the politically active have what the politically active think belongs to them. Christians should think in God's kingdom-encapsulated terms, not in human terms.

> Caesar could brand with his image coins, crowns, and robes, which moths would eat and rust would destroy. But life and creation have God's stamp on them. Caesar could have his coins, but life is God's. Caesar had no right to take what is God's. We are also reminded that just as Caesar stamped his image on coins, God's image is stamped on human beings.[4]

The political world means too much to Christianity, and people mean too little. Interestingly enough, I believe Warner would agree with that statement through his own views as well—the political world means too much to the GLBT community, and people mean too little.

Warner further confronts the plight of gays and lesbians who go against the grain. The trouble with normal, as his book title states, is that "the ones who pay are the ones who stand out in some way. They become a lightning rod not only for the hatred of difference, of the abnormal, but also for the more general loathing of sex."[5] His logic can also very clearly refer to the choice of GLBT people who decide to choose God over all else as a gay Christian, live as a celibate believer; or move toward a biblically traditional interpretation of sexuality—all of which stand out from the mainstream GLBT community. There is very real hostility and angst in the GLBT community's attitude toward ex-gay people and organizations. People who willfully leave behind same-sex sexual behavior are considered spineless conformists denying what God created them to be.

Think about how difficult a decision like that must be. It's giving up a life, a persona, an identity and more likely than not a group of friends and even an entire community. But in some small way, Christians can also understand what that is like. Warner's statement is applicable to what can happen with someone who intentionally steps out in faith from anything normally acceptable in Christian circles.

His associations also apply to the feeling that comes when new Christians profess their faith, or when someone "comes out" for the first time. The embrace of a new community or a new way of life, regardless of the spirit behind it, carries with it at least a perceived indictment of the status quo. The unique subsidiary effect to those "lighting rod experiences" is that, in and of themselves, they can bridge the gap between communities.

I once heard about an encounter between a man involved with Jews for Jesus and a newly out gay man. They bonded over the rejection they felt from the communities they grew up in, and the Jewish man went so far as to link both their stories to the gripping words of the Suffering Servant in Isaiah 53, who is Christ the crucified Lord.

He was oppressed and afflicted
yet he did not open his mouth. . . .
By oppression and judgment he was taken away. . . .
For he was cut off from the land of the living;
for the transgression of my people he was stricken.

Our Savior came as the ultimate lightning rod for the hatred of difference as he became the faultless model for those who are a part of the abnormal. He was despised and rejected, and still, his life made room for all of us who choose to walk a countercultural path. The beautiful struggle, and the compassion that flows from our Christ-centered hearts, is the same compassion that we have staked our entire life on, knowing that Jesus had that same compassion on us. It's time to start including into that compassion those people who many of us have thought to be the center of all things abnormal.

THE QUESTIONS CHRISTIANS CAN'T ANSWER

In 2006 I ran into my old high school baseball coach. What was an insignificant chance meeting at a restaurant gave me a clear and painful understanding of what was already ingrained in my own psyche. I explained that I started a nonprofit organization that works to build bridges between the GLBT and religious communities. He smiled at first and after taking a second to actually think about what I just said, he started to laugh so hard I thought he had misheard me!

When he was done laughing he said, "Do you remember what you used to say in high school?"

I couldn't remember, but I had a horrible feeling that I could guess what was coming.

"You used to call everyone a fag. And every other phrase out of your mouth was 'that's so gay!' I was a fag, other coaches were fags, teammates were fags, and your best friends were fags. Everyone was either a fag or gay."

Hearing what he said crippled me because his seemingly harmless memories of who I was really put everything in perspective. After almost seven years I was remembered not for my athletic accomplishments but for my free use of offensive and hurtful language. I never want anyone else to have to feel the shame I felt when a man I looked up to for four years in high school laughed in my face when I told him I was following God's command on my life—all because of who I used to be.

What bothered me most about this was that I didn't even know where any of my homophobic thoughts originated. I didn't remember hearing anything explicitly defaming gays or lesbians from either my church or my parents. But with many hours of difficult self-reflection, I started believing that general anti-gay thoughts are naturally just passed along within the broader Christian culture without us ever really realizing it's happening.

When I started working with middle- and high-school kids through The Marin Foundation, whenever I would hear a homophobic slur I would be sure to ask them right away where they got that from. Every single time their answer was the same: "I'm not sure. I've never thought about it before."

Chuck Colson says that *sin* is the most politically incorrect word in today's society, and he couldn't be more right. I define sin as anything that keeps one from realizing God's full and perfect potential. By that definition we are all sinners.

In today's cultural context, though, people outside the Christian community hear *sin* and automatically associate that with some type of Christian hierarchy based on hell and judgment. And since judgment is generally thought of negatively, sin is likewise seen as an intolerable negative—though not in the sense that Christians understand it to be. Believers understand sin to be a negative part of everyone's life. But the blood of Jesus, by way of his death on the cross, washed all past and future sins away and brought redemption through belief. Believers are able to overcome sin without having to be judged by it.

That is not the way the mainstream thinks of it. To them some inborn traits and characteristics can't just be washed away. Thus, it's believed, those certain unwashable things—physical, emotional or sexual—must not be "sin." We didn't have a choice of anything before we were born. We couldn't pick our family, our nationality, our social or economic status, our health or well-being, our skin color, or our inherent likes and dislikes. These things are part of who we are, and so we do not think of them in the category of "sin." The GLBT community would include in a list like this their sexual orientation. Ask yourself the following questions:

Why was I not chosen to have a same-sex attraction? Why was I born the way I was born? Why was I always sexually attracted to the other sex? Why was I not burdened with all that comes with being gay and lesbian? Why have I never had to entertain the idea of being celibate for my entire life? Why have I never had to think about fighting forever against a desire for sexual intimacy? Why am I me and not any of them? And why are they not me?

Are you entitled to your straightness? Are you blessed by God not to have to deal with same-sex attraction? You could have been gay. You could have been aborted and never had one memory of any existence you've lived to this point. You could have been anyone but you.

God is the only Creator and his will is beyond anything we could plan for ourselves. Heterosexual Christians take their sexuality as a birthright. I took it as a birthright until my eyes were opened by gays and lesbians who let me enter into their lives; living in their space I got to experience life with them in real-time.

Ron and I have known each other for a few years, and I have come to learn that he is probably the most well-thought-out person I have ever met. Ron will not say one word until he specifically thinks about exactly what will come out of his mouth, and the ramifications his words will cause. There are many people who spout off knee-jerk reactions to almost anything (I tend to be one of those people, and I promise I'm trying to work on it).

Ron attends a well-known evangelical church, and he began to tell me about a recent service. A video was played that had been recorded by a man a few months before he died. The man said that the five best days of his life were the day he met his wife, the day they got married and the day each of his three children were born. After the service Ron went up to the pastor with tears in his eyes and said, "If I continue to live the way that you're suggesting that I live [celibate], then I'll never experience any of the five best days that man experienced before his death."

The pastor paused as he looked Ron in the eyes and said, "I don't know what to tell you."

And then he moved on, and Ron went back to his car and cried.

I wish I had something profound to say to Ron when he told me this story. But I didn't. In sitting there with him all I kept thinking about was an eight-by-twelve-inch glass picture frame sitting on my desk; in it rests only one mustard seed. When I originally put the mustard seed in the frame I placed it in the middle of the frame so everyone could see how small a mustard seed really is. But when I closed the back of the frame the seed fell to the bottom left corner because it was too tiny to support itself. I tried to move it back in the middle for the next ten minutes, but after failing over and over I just gave up and let it stay in the bottom lefthand corner.

Without me planning it, that mustard seed teaches whoever happens upon my desk a valuable lesson. With puzzled looks people stare at the empty picture frame, then ask me why I would keep such a thing on my desk. I tell them that it's not empty and give it to them to look at more closely. When they see the tiny mustard seed in the bottom corner they get it. We are each mustard seeds—unable to establish ourselves, dependent on the intervention of Another, not in control of our circumstances but hopeful that God can bring us through them and establish the work of our hands.

I'm nothing and have nothing:
make something of me.
You can do it; you've got what it takes—
but God, don't put it off. (Ps 40:17 *The Message*)

More than anything I long for quick-fix answers for life's unanswerable questions. I pray the Lord will one day bring clarity to what so many—in both communities—deeply desire to comprehend. But that time is not now. Instead, I'm going to do what so many GLBT people have courageously done to me over the years: bare my soul.

THE DESIRE FOR SEXUAL INTIMACY

During college I didn't drink, I didn't smoke, I didn't do drugs, and I didn't swear. I was on regimented diets and work-out plans while playing baseball, and I had an ironclad willpower that could resist anything. Anything, that was, except girls who were attracted to me. I didn't have sex with them, but I did enough physically with them to know that how I was behaving was wrong.

Looking back I know my actions weren't an ego thing because I never told anyone. (If they were, I would have told everyone I knew.) I really think my actions were a yearning to express an intimacy that I felt I had to bury deep down inside because I was a Jesus-following believer.

Every time I would think to myself: *I could "struggle" with this, right?* It all eventually caught up to me and everything came out one night sitting on my bathroom floor, crying to my dad over the phone, apologizing for all that I did with those girls. I had filled my head with years of memories I didn't want to have anymore and I wanted more than anything to take it all back. But I couldn't. The only thing I could do was stop—so that night I stopped and told myself, nothing until I get married.

That was all in the past, and now I'm happily married. But those years of unwanted memories still haunt me today. I often wonder, did my behavior in the past make me a bad Christian? Not a Christian? Did they make me a Christian who just had strong desires for sexual intimacy and felt the need to express them through my ideal of love and sexuality?

They're tough questions, and to be honest I don't really like to think about the answers regardless of what they might be. Then I think of all the people I know in the GLBT community, and I think of all the celibate people I know who have a same-sex attraction, and then I think of all the gay Christians I know and wonder, do they emotionally, physically and spiritually go through what I went through? Do they feel what I felt? Is that what living in their shoes is like?

To build a bridge we have to make gays' and lesbians' situation real to us—just as Ron's pastor realized for the first time that he wasn't able to fill Ron's canyon of uncertainty. The pastor didn't have an answer to Ron's painful tears. I don't have an answer to them either. But I know God has an answer that will be revealed when the time is right for him to reveal it. And that will be the best answer to quench a longing to love, to be loved and to experience sexual intimacy.

My heart breaks for those who can't receive an answer to sexuality as easily as heterosexual Christians. I have spent many hours sitting and crying with friends, brothers, sisters or random acquaintances who struggle for any ounce of hope as they try with all of their fading might to figure out the "why" to every question that doesn't have an answer. It helps, when a person doesn't feel God's presence and isn't getting any of God's answers to such intimate struggles, to have someone in their corner fighting with them every step of the way—not someone fighting against them every step of the way. Gays and lesbians are searching for what we long for the most—good news from God.

Christians have to rely on the process, the journey, the nomadic discovery of searching for the Truth through God, alongside gays and lesbians. That is the only thing any of us can count on as a hope for stability in this existence, trying to understand our place on this earth. When the moment comes and you have to answer a crying, hurting person you care so deeply for, hurt and cry with them as you both embark on a new journey to walk side by side in discerning God's voice in their life.

6

Reclaiming the Word *Love*

Measurable Unconditional Behaviors

I hear from Christians all over the country that they feel a large disconnect between themselves and the GLBT community and yet have no idea what to do about it. This is as honest of a statement as I've heard; admitting that you don't know what to do is the same as knowing that you can't relate. And there is no better starting point than that.

There is a common thought that in any sport, coaches are allowed to be brash and mean and generally do whatever they see fit in order for a player to be built in the mold that the coach thinks best. To get to that malleable point, however, many coaches feel the player needs to first be torn down. I never thought that philosophy had any merit to it, and usually, it did more harm than good. In my experience, except for a select few players who responded to such treatment, coaches that followed the "tear down" philosophy got the worst out of their team as a whole. It didn't make sense to me when I was playing baseball, and it doesn't make sense to me in relation to the GLBT community either.

There are a number of Christian pastors, authors and activists who try to implement an athletic coach's "tear down" philosophy with the GLBT community because they think what they're doing will somehow end up benefiting gays and lesbians. And just like the coach's thought process, many Christians are hanging on with every ounce they have to the few GLBT people who respond favorably to such treatment—in their mind justifying the "tear down" approach. Well, it's not justified and actually does the broader gay and lesbian community more harm than good—continuing to widen the cultural divide as the few are generalized to the masses. Instead of continuing to diminish one side or the other, I concentrate on a new goal: reclaiming the word *love.* My goal is to explore how Christ's love manifests itself in believer's lives, and in turn, how to best express that love to the rest of the world.

THOSE WHO SEEK AND THOSE WHO DON'T

The traditional Christian approach to bridge building with gays and lesbians is what I call the 80-20 Reach. Keep in mind that pin-pointing structural percentages is impossible due to the number of people who have never told anyone about their same-sex attractions, but I believe that about 20 percent of the GLBT community is actively interested in ex-gay ministries and a change in orientation. That means on the flip side that *80 percent* of the GLBT community wants absolutely nothing to do with it.

I'm sure many gays and lesbians would say that 20 percent is way too high of a number. But whatever the breakdown, the point is still the same. An overwhelmingly large percentage of evangelical churches honestly believe they are doing significant bridge building work within the GLBT community because there are a couple gays and lesbians who actively seek them out for help. Christendom has been caught patting themselves on the back for working with the 20 percent of the GLBT community who sought them out.

What about the other remaining 80 percent—including those who consider themselves gay Christians? What are we doing to build a bridge to them? That's a lot of people we're talking about! I was recently in a meeting with a Christian who has extensively written about and researched ex-gay behavioral change. His claim is that there is as much as a 67 percent "success rate" (his words) for those GLBT people who participate in an ex-gay ministry. My question to him though: What happens to the other 33 percent of people who sought out and participated in the ex-gay ministry and "failed" (his words)? After much prodding as he continued to talk around the question he finally admitted the answer. "Nothing—we don't have any follow-up and we don't know what happens to them after they leave [or fail]."

Extend that logic to other missions of the church: is it OK if the church only reaches 20 percent of the rest of the world and is completely comfortable ignoring or fighting against the other 80 percent? The church isn't OK with 20 percent of anything, except maybe as a tithe check. (Just kidding.) The other 80 percent are easily dismissed as people who are either too odd, too risky to handle or too much of a failure.

In the groundbreaking book *unChristian,* based off of a research project looking into the way sixteen-to-twenty-nine-year-old non-Christians view Christians, the three most common perceptions of present-day Christians are that they are anti-gay (91 percent), judgmental (87 percent) and hypocritical (85 percent).[1]

I don't understand why Christians are so surprised when they finally figure that out. As soon as you decide to call yourself a Christian, a believer, a follower of Jesus—you are automatically held to a different, very skeptical, higher standard. The whole premise of Christianity is to hold oneself to a higher standard, above what others would think is culturally "normal." The research in *unChristian* shows that for the last couple of decades Christians have been starting from behind the eight-ball within the mainstream—especially within the GLBT community. But that doesn't mean we can't regain the lost ground by starting today to prove ourselves otherwise.

FITTING A ROUND PEG INTO A SQUARE HOLE

This past winter I caught the stomach flu, and when it hit me, it hit hard and fast and left me in a world of hurt. For the first few days I felt sorry for myself as my body had to endure the suffering of not being able to keep anything down, not being able to sleep and, on top of that, having a fever of over 100 degrees. In the midst of this pain though, my mind kept wandering back to Jeff.

Jeff is dying of AIDS. I couldn't shake the image of his face staring me in the eyes. I couldn't stop thinking about him—and death. As if I'd wandered into a hazy dream, I imagined standing over Jeff's casket thinking of all of the times that we were supposed to get together during the long winter months, during the allergy-ridden spring, during the blazing hot and humid summer, during the irregular shifting temperatures of a Chicago fall. However, far too often Jeff couldn't leave his house for the fear of catching a simple cold. Each sickness or infection he gets, regardless of its severity, can potentially be lethal. Emergency room visits and a continual series of tubes injecting who knows what into his body are the only answers to try to escape the unwanted grasp of death's arms. Even so, none of it matters. Jeff knows what is going to kill him one day.

It was this same Jeff who a few months earlier sat before me crying, telling me about his life before AIDS. His words are imprinted in my soul as he quivered and said, "I didn't have to be dying right now."

I know Jeff could tell that I had no clue what he was saying. After a minute of silence as he held his head in his hands Jeff looked at me and said:

> You know, I wouldn't be dying if someone could have just told me it would have been OK for me to just be me. That I didn't have to sleep around and get girls pregnant like my brothers. That I didn't have to get married like my sisters. That I didn't have to do stuff with guys just because I was attracted to them. That I could express my love to God without doing anything that I was expected to do from either side.
>
> I could have just been me. If someone would have just told me any of that, I wouldn't be dying right now. No one can ever know what it's like to know what is going to kill you one day. I shouldn't have known this either.

We could have saved his life. His family could have saved his life. His church could have saved his life. His gay friends and partners could have saved his life. I feel like I should save his life now. But I can't. I can only be there to try to take away some of death's pain as I watch him deteriorate into that casket that I vividly imagined in my dream.

Both communities—GLBT and Christian—hold responsibility for making sure that Jeff's story is never repeated. If both sides could stop pressuring their own to be someone they're not, to do something they don't want to do, and stop trying to continually fit a round peg into a square hole, Jeff's life can eventually live on through the lives of those who will never have to go through what he does.

From a straight Christian perspective, the ideal life is to get married and have a family. From a gay perspective the ideal is to come out and live a happy, sexually reconciled faith as an active gay man or lesbian woman. And for those believers with a same-sex attraction who don't fit in the other two ideals, the third ideal is to be celibate. What each ideal has in common is that they all focus on sex—or lack thereof—as the standard by which to judge a life.

What about people like Jeff? Jeff doesn't see himself as a part of the GLBT community or the Christian community he grew up in. He doesn't want to continue feeling pressured to come out and deal with it. If not that, the only other "respectable" option is to choose to live void of sexual intimacy. People like Jeff get lost in the social and religious utopia each community's ideals presume. Therefore in Jeff's mind, and in the minds of many other people I know, it is better for them to go on the "down-low"—a very destructive pattern of hiding their same-sex attractions from the outside world, while acting on them in secret.

There's a fourth ideal that gets overlooked, an ideal that is not based on sex: It's OK to be yourself before God and not conform to any of the other three ways that seem ideal to the outside world.

The fourth ideal communicates God's acceptance, validation, affirmation and unconditional love in meeting people as they are, where they are. Some critics might think this fourth ideal is the same as a blanket acceptance of the gay identity. Others might think this fourth ideal is the same as celibacy, just renamed to try to make it more accessible. But the fourth ideal is rooted in neither. It's an ideal focused on an identity in Christ rather than behavior—straight, gay or celibate—as the judge of one's acceptability.

The fourth ideal says that an ideal existence is one that does not have to accept or conform to any sexual personification that mainstream society (secular or religious) deems as the only means to a normal existence. The totality of an individual's worth, instead of the significance of a behavior, gives straight Christians, GLBT people and those in between room to elevate the conversation by deconstructing the overhyped value of sexual behavior. We must allow people to consider God unencumbered by the blinders of a forced sexual identity—in either direction. Without that room many people like Jeff will continue to get lost in this world's Christian and secular ideological expectations of spiritualized sexuality as the standard of what is desired.

WHY ONE-WORD ANSWERS?

The fourth ideal is a good example of a principle I've discovered in my relationships with GLBT people: if you change the questions, you inevitably change the conversation. Whenever I speak at GLBT events across the country, it never fails that the very first question I am always asked is, "Do you think homosexuality is a sin?" Whenever I speak at Christian events the very first question I am always asked is, "Do you think that gays and lesbians can change?" The most common questions I receive in any venue are always closed-ended—asking me for a short, opinionated closed-ended response. After seeing this pattern repeat itself over a lengthy amount of time I felt the need to examine the motives behind such a universally accepted means to query someone's belief system.

Closed-ended questions are made to be answered with a "yes" or "no." John Richardson Jr., a professor of information studies at

UCLA, states that closed-ended questions "discourage disclosure."
Such questions

> can include presuming, probing, or leading questions . . . can
> be leading and hence irritating or even threatening to user,
> can result in misleading assumptions/conclusions about the
> user's information need.[2]

Closed-ended questions don't cultivate dialogue. The asker has
already answered the question for themselves and is only seeking
to figure out where the other person fits within their own precon-
ceived metric—either for or against. Even the most well-intentioned
people routinely ask closed-ended, opinion-based questions in an
attempt to grasp who you are, what you believe and which camp
you should be placed in. And the yes or no responses to those in-
quiries quickly trigger a predetermined set of thoughts, beliefs
and rebuttals already in place for a yes answer—as well a different
set of predetermined thoughts, beliefs and rebuttals already in
place for a no answer.

How backwards is that—that a one-word answer to the most divisive topic in the church today is universally accepted as the normal
way to handle such controversy? Closed-ended questions reflect a
dichotomized belief system that tears people apart. They breed segregation in an us versus them mindset rather than give an opportunity for productive bridge building. My first rule of thumb, therefore, is to never answer a closed-ended question with a closed-ended
answer! I instead change the question to an open-ended version and
ask right back.

The way I handle such a situation is not a new response—just a
forgotten one. Jesus modeled this practice throughout the Gospels.
One such famous conversation happened between Jesus and the
Pharisees as they tried to trap him about paying taxes to Caesar.
Knowing full well the simplistic answer to their question, Jesus
did not respond with yes or no but rather elevated the conversation
with a question of his own that more thoroughly made his point.

Jesus understood the intentionality that many of the hot-button legalistic issues of his day deserved—just as the topic of homosexuality deserves today. Realizing that one-word answers would only feed into the growing disconnect between the movement of the Way and the religious systems of the past, Jesus took another approach—an approach that provided space for an in-depth understanding.

When two older gay men pulled me to the side at my evening Bible study and told me that they had left their gay-affirming church and were treating our time together as their church, I was confused. Why would they leave a church that told them that they were born that way and their sexual behaviors are not a sin, in favor of a Bible study held by a college student who is a conservative Bible-believing evangelical? Not only that, but they went so far as to tell their GLBT friends to talk to me as well. Without knowing what else to do I stood in front of the group that next week and asked two questions:

"Why do you come?"

"Why do you tell others to come?"

I went around the room one by one. The two main answers they gave me have shaped not only how I run The Marin Foundation, but also gave a unique insight into how Christians are able to productively build a bridge. First, they told me they keep coming back because, "When you don't feel fine inside, you can only be told you're fine for so long." The people in attendance said that the gay-affirming churches they had attended in the past focus intently on sexuality—sometimes to a fault. Whatever Scripture was being studied—even when another issue was the focused subject matter—somehow, sexuality was spiritualized alongside it. Those GLBT people in the group related that the Bible study was a breath of fresh air because I didn't focus on their sexuality at all; instead, I unapologetically focused on how to have a better, more intimate relationship with God apart from any GLBT issues.

I did that on purpose—not because I had some intelligent master plan but because I was too scared to say anything about sexuality! I was still trying to work through all of those questions myself, and the last thing I wanted to do was say the wrong thing and create a mass gay and lesbian exodus. I knew the Bible. I knew the Lord. I didn't know homosexuality. So I just stuck with what I knew.

The other thing that I didn't understand was, why did the people in attendance encourage other gays and lesbians to attend as well? Their answer was closely related to the first, yet also totally separate: "You treat us like children of God and not gays and lesbians who want to be Christians." They told me that if they were to walk into any type of church, regardless of their intentions, they would expect to be either made fun of or put on display as the token gay people to prove the church's diversity. Many of the gays and lesbians who came were intrigued that I was a straight guy who wanted to have this group, and not a gay pastor who teaches gay theology or an ex-gay person attempting to share their "freedom" experience.

There is a true thirst within the broader GLBT community to know the God who shut the lions' mouths when Daniel was thrown into their den; to know the God who kept Shadrach, Meshach and Abednego from having one hair burned when they were cast into a furnace; to know the God who wrote his Son into the story to save his beloved children. That Bible study would not have grown if GLBT people didn't want it. The Marin Foundation would not continue to grow in the GLBT community if they didn't want it. The fight between GLBT-Christian issues would not persist so strongly if GLBT people didn't want to find some way to reconcile themselves to the Almighty.

I started to realize that the gay and lesbian community was more than just a sexual behavior. They were children of God, and longed to be looked at and validated as such. And so with all of the dignity and respect I have for myself, for them and for my Father, that is exactly what I do.

WHAT DO YOU MEAN, CHANGE?

A few weeks after the original conversation with those two gay men, I started to have handfuls of people from the group come to me on the side and tell me, "God is telling me that I'm not gay, and I need your help."

What!? Where did that come from? I had intentionally never talked about "change" so why were they approaching me with these thoughts? They said, "That's the point. You didn't tell me anything. God did."

These people were a very small percentage of the larger group, but they nonetheless led me to conclude that the more persistently Christians help GLBT people connect with God's voice, the more regularly crazy things happen. I've seen with my own two eyes God at work on his time in his rightful place—as his plan is always bigger (and more confusing) than our own. I'll never understand kingdom ways or methods. I might be able to pick up a pattern or trend here or there, but actual implementation is beyond any of us. That is why finding the best way from gay to straight doesn't matter to me. In fact, I believe that the topics of homosexuality, "change" or sexuality in general aren't even the main issues. The main issue is how we as followers of Christ are to live in relation to, and relationship with, the GLBT community. Since being in relation to and relationship with gays and lesbians are the only two things we can faithfully control, those are the two means that I root my heart and soul within.

PROJECT RECLAIMING THE WORD *LOVE*

One summer evening, I was reading an interview with Billy Graham's daughter. She was telling some of her fondest memories about her dad and recalled one time in particular, when the Graham family was attending a rally in support of President Bill Clinton after his sex scandal was made public. A reporter asked Billy Graham, "Why are you here supporting this man after everything he has done to this country?"

Reverend Graham's answer was succinct, powerful and true. "It is the Holy Spirit's job to convict, God's job to judge and my job to love."

When I read that sentence I started to cry because it just put words to what I had unknowingly been doing within the GLBT community since my immersion began. It's not the job of Christians to convict the GLBT community. That's the Holy Spirit's job. It's not the job of Christians to judge the GLBT community. That's God's job. It's the job of Christians to love the GLBT community in a way that is tangible, measurable and unconditional—whether we see our version of "change" happening or not!

That realization has led to my new definition of love: tangible and measurable expressions of one's unconditional behaviors toward another. My experience has revealed that in the minds of GLBT people, the word *love* has been rendered conditional: "I will love you if I see you do . . . , or act like . . . , or sexually change . . ." Someone can say the words "I love you" until that person is blue in the face, but it will not matter one bit unless there are measurable, unconditional behaviors attached to those words. My friends, my wife and my family will know that I love them not because I say so but because I show who I am *to* them by what I do *for* them.

This revised definition of love entails that Christians be committed to a love that gives the recipient something that they can hold on to as a representation of that feeling. Christians must understand the gravity of the situation in how a person's sexual orientation relates to their potential faith. Words cannot regain what has been lost through the many negative perceptions of Christian people. The only way for gays and lesbians to believe what Christians profess about love is through tangible, measurable and unconditional behaviors that speak for themselves.

What do these tangible, measurable and unconditional behaviors look like? They are a nonjudgmental safe place—an environment that fosters a trustworthy relationship with someone else. Love is a walk, a hug, a dinner, an ear, a fun trip—all free of the condemning and ostracizing that the GLBT person "knows" is coming from

Christians. This type of love says that no matter who you are, no matter what you do or no matter what you say I have your back, and I refuse to give up—whether or not there's "change"—because my Father will never give up on me.

The biblical basis for love is rooted in patience, kindness, truth, righteousness, hope, compassion and *endurance* (1 Cor 13; Gal 5:6; Col 1:5; 1 Pet 4:7-11).

> Love, as set forth by Jesus, is the keynote of the new kingdom. It is also the epitome of the Old Testament ethic. The obligation to love extends not only to one's relatives, not only to one's neighbor, but even to one's enemies . . . [as] the positive reaction of love [is] expressed in deeds.[3]

Despite what many believe, true biblical love does not come naturally to our human nature. It is not natural for us to get hit on the right cheek and then turn to the abuser the other cheek as well. It is not natural for us to earnestly forgive those who continue to purposefully wrong us seventy times seven times. It is not natural for us to literally love our neighbor, brother or enemy exactly and perfectly how we love ourselves. I don't know one person—including myself—who consistently does any of those things. And yet that is God's definitive word on how he wants us to represent our faith through love.

The Bible is full of stories that teach us how to love, instead of just giving us instructions on how to verbally communicate love. Love is to be an action—not a word. Love is recognizing the power of Christ to do what we could only imagine, like physically going to him with the faith of a Roman centurion—greater than all other faith in Israel. Love is stepping outside the boat to meet your Savior by walking on water, when every ounce of your body is telling you otherwise. Love is boldly pouring expensive perfume on Jesus' feet when indeed, the poor could have benefited from the money of its potential sale. Love is cutting a hole in a roof and lowering your crippled friend to Jesus when there are no other accessible means to the one who can heal. Love is a poor widow dropping all she has—two very small copper coins worth nothing—into God's treasury with no guarantee she'll make it another day. Love is stepping out of all cultural norms to help a beaten-up man lying on the side of the street, despite the fact that his culture despises yours. And love is being the first one to drop the stone because you know your life and sins are no less than any other.

The one thing all of these examples have in common is that they're acts of love around Jesus, not acts of Jesus himself. We have the power to counterculturally love through our tangible, measurable and unconditional actions louder than any words could ever be spoken—as Jesus is ever presently there with us in the gay, lesbian, bisexual and transgender community. Christians are to be characterized by loving all comers, not just those who love us. And just to prove the Almighty was not about talk, but of actions, he sent his Son as the ultimate expression of love.

You see, at just the right time, when we were still powerless, Christ died for the ungodly. Very rarely will anyone die for a righteous man, though for a good man someone might possibly dare to die. But God demonstrates his own love for us in this: While we were still sinners, Christ died for us. (Rom 5:6-8)

Committing to love others tangibly, measurably and unconditionally is a fearful proposition, but one we must move forward in nonetheless. What if a GLBT person says, "I have felt your love and listened to God as you have showed me, and God told me it's OK to be gay"? Fear of the "what-ifs" tends to have a strong crippling effect on Christians' outlook and practice. But we're not called to live in fear; we're called to live in faith one day at a time.

I strongly believe that whenever Jesus is involved, change is soon to follow. I'm not necessarily talking about sexual orientation; I'm talking about mind, soul and eternal understanding. Lives change with Jesus, and if a GLBT person says that God has indicated that it's OK to be gay, the Christian community has to deeply trust and rely on the knowledge that we can never know the end to God's best journey for someone else's life. A man named Rob is a real-life example.

Rob was raised in an evangelical home and loved the Lord with all his heart. When he realized at the age of twenty-three that he was attracted to other men, he did as so many others do—prayed, fasted and sought help. Nothing seemed to work, as Rob's attractions continued to grow stronger each day. One day when he was praying he very clearly felt that God was telling him that it was OK that he was gay, and that he had the freedom to explore his sexual desires.

Rob couldn't wait to tell me, so he called me up and gave me a word-by-word rundown of the entire conversation. I reminded him to keep his spirit open to hearing what the Lord would continue to say, even after that point. The moment someone limits God's voice to only one way to accomplish their prayers, whatever the prayer, is the same moment that person has just tried to force God onto their timetable. I firmly believe that no matter if Rob's insight was good or bad, or right or wrong—each piece of the journey needs to happen as is, in order to get to the next phase in God's mysterious plan. As we hung up he felt free at last from the hatred he had been heaping on himself for so many years, and he joyfully immersed himself into the GLBT community.

Five years later Rob was still riding high on God's revelation to him. In a solid two-year relationship with another man, he felt truly happy for the first time in his life. But in the sixth year Rob started to feel another tug on his life. His relationship deteriorated, and when they broke up he began looking for another man to share his life with. But the thought of having to try to impress someone all over again was just too much of a daunting burden. He looked around at many of the older gay men he knew who were still trying to find someone and all Rob saw was lonely person after lonely person. Confused, he again started to pray, fast and ask God to help him through whatever was happening.

As clearly as Rob heard God tell him it was OK for him to be gay, he heard God tell him "that it was time for you to come back to me." Rob had been so narrowly focused on his gay sexuality that God gave him what he wanted—the release to explore his same-sex attractions. Rob told me after, "God knew I would never have been able to move forward in his will unless I experienced everything for myself because I would have never been fully committed to him, wondering, 'what if?'" Heeding God's call, Rob started down a new path and now is living a solidified life again focused on God—not on what he feels he needs to be sexually.

There are also many others like Rob whose original conclusion doesn't change in five, ten or forty years. Even though there are GLBT people who are convinced throughout the course of their lives that God told them they're GLBT, it doesn't give Christians the right to give up and start reverting back to the old way of handling things. Christians need to be reminded of Matthew 7:21-23 in which Jesus says,

> Not everyone who says to me, "Lord, Lord," will enter the kingdom of heaven, but only he who does the will of my Father who is in heaven. Many will say to me on that day, "Lord, Lord, did we not prophesy in your name, and in your name drive out demons and perform many miracles?" Then I will tell them plainly, "I never knew you. Away from me, you evildoers!"

Neither I, nor you, nor anyone else other than the Father knows each person's true heart and soul. Far be it that the Christian community becomes so cocky in their standing that they think they know eternal judgments at heaven's gates. R. T. France puts it masterfully in his commentary on the aforementioned passage:

> We are introduced to those who apparently believe themselves to be genuine disciples and can appeal to their charismatic activities to prove it, but nonetheless turn out to have no real relationship with the *Lord* to whom they appeal. . . . [T]hese [claiming Christians] are self-deceived. Acceptance depends not on profession, nor even on apparently Christian activity, but on whether Jesus *knew* them. Note the extraordinary au-

thority he assumes as judge; *to enter the kingdom of heaven* depends on his acknowledgment and consists in being with him.[4]

We just never know, do we? Let it all be in the Lord's hands and plan as he sees it to be good. He is taking all of us through a journey in which we can't see the next turn. As I always keep it in my mind: It's the Holy Spirit's job to convict, God's job to judge, and our job to love gays and lesbians in tangible and measurable ways through our unconditional behaviors as a flesh representation of Jesus Christ in their lives—no matter what the outcome.

7

The Big 5

Principles for a More Constructive Conversation

Homosexuality and the Bible. What a topic. Go to Amazon, Borders, Barnes & Noble or any of the Christian bookstores and see the hundreds of books that have been written on the topic all claiming the same thing: the author knows what the Bible *really* says about homosexuality.

I recently went to Amazon.com and did a search on homosexuality and the Bible, and up popped 1,577 books that referenced this topic. I started to count how many books were written from each perspective. I found that out of the first 107 books, 60 of them argue that the Bible definitively supports homosexuality and allows for monogamous and committed same-sex relationships. The other 47 advocate a traditional Christian hermeneutical interpretation against same-sex sexual behavior of any kind. And then I gave up counting—I got the point.

As far back as the very first book in the Bible, some people thought that same-sex sexual behavior was OK, and some thought it wasn't. So it's not a big shocker to me that the same difference in opinion still exists today. The argument surrounds five texts:

- Genesis 19—the Sodom and Gomorrah story

- Leviticus 18:22 and 20:13—sections of the Holiness Code that prohibit same-sex sexual behavior and list the punishments for those behaviors

- Romans 1:26-27—determining what is sexually natural and unnatural

- 1 Corinthians 6:9-11—same-sex sexual behavior's non-inclusion to the kingdom of God

- 1 Timothy 1:9-11—the need for sound doctrine in opposition to false teachers of the law; condemning same-sex sexual behavior as part of a larger group

There it is. Two passages in the Old Testament and three passages in the New Testament that each clearly speak to the topic of homosexuality. The fun begins when we ask what they all mean to us today.

Maybe there are times when my vivid imagination gets the best of me, and this might be one of them, but I can't help picturing each community as rivals in the play *West Side Story.* Both sides round up their friends to rendezvous in a back alley for a street brawl/dance-off. Corny, isn't it? And as ridiculous as that piece of imagery is, it's the same ridiculousness I feel when it comes to the roundabout way in which both communities seem to continually go back and forth when it comes to biblical interpretation. Both communities can talk around the crux of their argument as much as they want, add as much persuasive fluff as deemed necessary or scientifically detail "new" information. Instead, I think it's time we elevated our hermeneutics.

BIBLICAL INTERPRETATION

The interpretation of Greek and Hebrew terms in the Bible is central to the debates over homosexuality. Ultimately biblical interpretation informs cultural application on both sides. But what did the biblical writers intend their words to mean to their original audience? Dr. David Woodall, professor of biblical hermeneutics and Greek in the graduate school at Moody Bible Institute, says that precise biblical interpretation is dependent upon accurately crossing the cultural bridge from the biblical times to our current culture. So I'm going to briefly detail my hermeneutical process.

The New Testament, according to *Grasping God's Word* by J. Scott Duvall and J. Daniel Hays, is appropriately interpreted in four steps:

1. What did the text mean to the biblical audience?

2. What are the cultural, language, situational, time and covenant differences between the biblical audience and Christians today?

3. What is the overarching principle in the text?

4. How are Christians today able to best apply the overarching theological principle in their lives?

The Old Testament has the same steps as the New Testament, with one addition: the overarching Old Testament principle must be considered against a New Testament context before it is applied to contemporary life. The Old Testament law was originally written for the Israelites who lived under the old covenant. Therefore old covenant laws and regulations can be applicable to our current culture only after being filtered through their own time period's hermeneutical grid.[1]

Application for Old Testament laws, then, is about the principles laid forth for all eternity that have crossed over to New Testament, new covenant teachings—not about the exact words written on the page. Through such an understanding, *all* of the Old Testament still applies to new covenant Christians by way of principles always applicable in any time period or generation (Mk 13:31).

The main question then: What constitutes a qualifying eternal principle from Scripture?

1. The principle should be reflected in the biblical text.

2. The principle should not be tied to a specific situation.

3. The principle should not be culturally bound to a specific date, time, situation or group of people.

4. The principle should correspond to the teaching of the rest of Scripture.

5. The principle should be relevant to both biblical and contemporary audiences.[2]

The typical pattern of interpretational fights between the GLBT and Christian communities begins over specific Greek and Hebrew terms, then works its way out through the verse, then the passage, then the chapter and then the book, to ultimately determine the significance of a passage.

However, the key to biblical interpretation is to work in the opposite direction: to start with the book and then move to the chapter, to the passage, to the verse and then to the specific words. This way the hotly contested words already have a context and do not become a historic, culturally bound definition that many attempt to generalize to the current culture.

Nine years ago when my best friends came out to me I had no idea how to reconcile my conservative beliefs and their sexual behaviors. I started grabbing onto anything I could get that might give me some optimism. My goal was not to just look for contrary beliefs so I could justify my best friends, but rather to really try for the first time to take an objective look at homosexuality and what I believe. My theological search led me to some strange places—on both sides.

But all things considered, I knew that whatever I was to find in the Bible was to be my final answer about my friends and their sexual orientation. And that frightened me. I didn't want to be left with no choice but to alienate my best friends. I was, however, also very aware of the fact that my concern for my friendships might cloud my interpretation. The Bible tells us not to add or subtract anything, and I was scared to death of doing just that. So I started at the only place I thought would give me answers, right at the main passages that speak to homosexuality.

Looking back, I realize that my naiveté about the issue greatly helped me out. The more I read and studied those passages in their

118 LOVE IS AN ORIENTATION

broader context with an eye to the overarching lessons about what is being described about God and his will for our lives, the more clearly I saw an emerging set of eternal principles on how to seek God more intently. I learned that what had always been used as the same old "gay-bashing" passages can instead build a bridge that allows GLBT people to draw near to God. These principles are not just yeses or nos, nor are they just about sexuality. They are *the* formula to learn how to know God better—in a more real way than ever before.

MIND-FRAME-SHIFT PRINCIPLE: GENESIS 19

One of the main keys to biblical interpretation is being able to hone in on parallel passages in other parts of Scripture that speak to the same theme or main point of the desired passage. When we ask why Sodom and Gomorrah were destroyed in Genesis 19, we can find some insight in Ezekiel 16:49-50.

> Now this was the sin of your sister Sodom: She and her daughters were arrogant, overfed and unconcerned; they did not help the poor and needy. They were haughty and did detestable things before me. Therefore I did away with them as you have seen.

Sodom and Gomorrah are described as overfed, unconcerned, nonjustice-minded people who tried to potentially and literally rape their guests—all of which are in direct opposition to the very strict hospitality laws of the Old Testament days. None of the themes in Ezekiel 16 are even remotely close to resembling the committed monogamous same-sex relationships we know of today. Because of that, pro-gay theologians assert that the overarching theme to Genesis 19 is not homosexuality.

The battleground is thus set as the debate over whether Sodom was destroyed because of homosexuality, rape or inhospitality. It's a question of interpreting the Hebrew word *yadah*, traditionally defined as "to know" or "to engage in sex." This single focus restricts the conversation to the word level, neglecting the more important prior interpretive principles: from Testament to book to chapter to verse.

There is another parallel passage to the Sodom and Gomorrah story that always gets overlooked, but its meaning is as clear as a cloudless sky: "Remember Lot's wife! Whoever tries to keep his life will lose it, and whoever loses his life will preserve it" (Lk 17:32-33). Here Jesus is discussing the coming kingdom of God with his disciples, after the Pharisees questioned him about it. Jesus' words about what happens when one keeps or loses their life is an illustration of the main point: Lot's wife, *the* example of what not to do when it comes to entering the kingdom of God.

Step back for a second and think about how the GLBT community fits into the broader picture of an eternal principle regarding life and their ability to enter the kingdom of God. Ask most any Christian what the main point to Sodom and Gomorrah is, and they'll say homosexuality. But Jesus had something else in mind. He used the Sodom and Gomorrah story by specifically pointing out Lot's wife to indicate what's involved in entering the kingdom.

The story thus begins not in Genesis 19 but in Genesis 13, when Abram and his nephew Lot grow so wealthy and numerous that they can no longer stay together. Abram gives Lot the first choice of where each of them will live, and Lot chooses for himself the fertile land of Sodom over the dry plains of Canaan.

Sodom was located near the well-watered Jordan Valley of the Dead Sea, and because of its strategic location to a large mass of water, it was thriving economically. Sodom was luxurious and prosperous, and therefore Lot thought it would be easier to quickly thrive in his soon-to-be new existence there, than to trust God to provide for his needs in the destitute dry plains.

The first verse of Genesis 19 tells us that the angels arrived at Sodom and met Lot who was sitting in the gateway—an indication that Lot was a businessman and a cue to his place of prominence in the city.[3] Lot's home and possessions in Sodom are not mentioned outside of the original assessment of his prosperity in Genesis 13, but an already wealthy man who goes to a richly established city and becomes a prominent member of their community as an alien to that land speaks for itself regarding the life Lot and his family lived in Sodom. They were living the high life.

Lot's wife is first mentioned briefly in verse 15 when the angels command Lot to take his family out of Sodom before it's destroyed. We don't hear from her again until verse 26 when she becomes a pillar of salt. But there is still much to take from this one verse. Whenever I read this story my imagination takes over. I picture Lot, his wife and his daughters running at a dead sprint through Sodom's busy streets as everyone in the city is trying to escape the burning sulfur slowly moving its way from one end of Sodom to the other. Lot and his family escape to the dry plains, but his wife starts to slow down and lag behind.

"No, no! What are you doing? We must keep going until we reach Zoar. Come on!"

Lot's wife doesn't want to leave. She doesn't want to see all of her wonderful possessions melt away into nothing. She doesn't want to go back to her old life. Lot and his daughters drag her the rest of the way to Zoar, and upon their arrival Lot's wife is suicidal and so angry that her husband would force her out of her amenity-filled life in Sodom. "I would have rather died in Sodom than have to come here with you!" And with that Lot's wife storms away and sprints to the highest place she can find to look, and cry, one more time to reminisce about what she had in Sodom.

The moment she reaches her high place, she gazes upon the smoke that was once her home. God sees her loving this destroyed place with a love he longs for her to have only for him. And so he gives Lot's wife to her darling Sodom, and she shares in its fate.

Craig Keener observes that "when Lot's wife looked back to her destroyed home in Sodom, it cost her her life, which had been of greater value to God than her possessions."[4] Her "attachment to earthly things," observes I. Howard Marshall, cost her the life that God had so joyfully prepared for her.[5]

The story of Lot's wife and Sodom and Gomorrah teaches us that until people (straight and GLBT) learn to shift their own mind frame from earthly issues, there can never be any forward movement in a personal relationship with Jesus. Straight and GLBT people alike can look at Sodom and Gomorrah for what they were, as mentioned in Ezekiel: arrogant, overfed, unconcerned, haughty, detestable and all in all inhospitable. But the greater point that Jesus made to his disciples as he elevated the Sodom and Gomorrah story was that regardless of what the people of Sodom did, nothing was more tragic than a person turning her back on Almighty God to yearn for things manmade.

The same is true in another relevant Old Testament example. In 1 Kings 14:7-9 the prophet Ahijah related the following message to Jeroboam's death:

> [The Lord] raised you [Jeroboam] up from among the people and made you a leader over my people Israel. I tore the kingdom away from the house of David and gave it to you, but you have not been like my servant David, who kept my commands and followed me with all his heart, doing only what was right in my eyes. You have done more evil than all who lived before you. You have made for yourself other gods, idols made of metal; you have provoked me to anger and thrust me behind your back.

I find it interesting that repeated throughout the Old Testament after David's death, the Lord gives to prophets the words that keep referring to David as "a man who followed God's commands and followed him with all his heart, doing only what was right in God's eyes." Isn't this the same David who impregnated Bathsheba and killed her husband so no one would find out? Yes. But God is giving us insight into how he sees our hearts through kingdom standards. David committed a behavioral sin, and suffered consequences for it. But Jeroboam committed a spiritual sin, turning his heart away from the Lord by making himself gods and idols of metal. David is remembered as the one who did what was right in God's eyes, and Jeroboam is remembered as the one who did more evil than any who lived before him.

The kingdom of God is not for those who have lived a perfect life on earth. The kingdom of God is rather for those who have shifted their mind frame away from earthly things and onto God, seeking God to help them do all in their human ability to follow him rather than turning their backs on him. Recognizing the eternal importance of seeking God above everything else rather than debating orientation, sex or politics is the first eternal principle of bridge building with gays and lesbians.

CROSSROADS PRINCIPLE: THE HOLINESS CODE

The next set of passages that speak to homosexuality are found in Leviticus 18:22 and 20:13.

Do not lie with a man as one lies with a woman; that is detestable.

If a man lies with a man as one lies with a woman, both of them have done what is detestable. They must be put to death; their blood will be on their own heads.

When it comes to the book of Leviticus both communities are solely focused once again on the debates of word meaning. The major issues stem over the Hebrew words *shakab* and *toevah*, traditionally translated in Leviticus 18:22 as "to lie with" and "detestable (abomination)." But something more significant is being communicated within the Holiness Code.

The Holiness Code, another name for Leviticus 17—26, defined God's rules to the Israelites in order to maintain their holiness as well as their distinctiveness from the rest of the world as God's chosen people. Today many non-Christians, and even many Christians, find the Holiness Code a bit ridiculous. But just as Jesus' life was countercultural in comparison to the New Testament times, so was the Holiness Code used as God's way to directly confront the social norms and constructs of the Old Testament culture. This is emphasized by the phrase "I am the LORD your God," repeated over thirty times throughout Leviticus.

In order to understand the overarching Crossroads Principle we must understand how the parallel chapters of Leviticus 18 and 20 are constructed. The first verse in the Holiness Code that speaks to homosexuality is 18:22. Chapter 18 starts off the fourth subsection of the book of Leviticus (18:1–27:34), detailing God's commands of how the people of Israel are to tangibly live their lives for God as a separated, chosen people, in direct opposition to how the Canaanites lived and worshiped. So the beginning of Leviticus 18 sets the tone for the entire Israelite community as they are to understand all of the practical applications to follow.

This pivotal chapter is broken down into three distinct sections: introduction (vv. 1-5), body (vv. 6-23) and conclusion (vv. 24-30). The introduction sets up the body; the body expands on what was introduced; and the conclusion reiterates the main point of the body, often overlapping the content of the introduction. Leviticus 18:2-5 says,

> I am the LORD your God. You must not do as they do in Egypt, where you used to live, and you must not do as they do in the land of Canaan, where I am bringing you. Do not follow their practices. You must obey my laws and be careful to follow my decrees. I am the LORD your God. Keep my decrees and laws, for the man who obeys them will live by them. I am the LORD.

The main point to this introduction, and subsequently to the broader focus of all that follows, is that God is Lord and the Israelites were not to do as the Egyptians or the Canaanites did. The contextual body that directly follows this introduction is a series of nineteen consecutive "do not" rules that outline exactly how the Egyptians and Canaanites religiously practiced, including verse 22 about homosexuality. The conclusion comes in verses 25-30, warning the Israelites not to follow any of the customs they had come in contact with outlined in the body; otherwise the same fate would happen to them as was going to happen to the Canaanites.

This gives us an insightful moment of foreshadowing what is to come in the next verse that speaks to homosexuality: Leviticus 20:13. The construction of chapter 20 details the punishments for following the ways of the Egyptians and Canaanites listed in the body of chapter 18. There are five main types of punishments handed out by God in chapter 20, and it's important to remember that these punishments (including being cut off from the Israelites, and death) cannot be literally generalized to Christians today because we are under a new covenant—but the theme of the punishments is still to be taken very seriously. The conclusion to chapter 20 rightfully sums up these two parallel chapters:

> "Keep all my decrees and laws and follow them, so that the land where I am bringing you to live may not vomit you out. You must not live according to the customs of the nations I am going to drive out before you. Because they did all these things, I abhorred them. But I said to you, "You will possess their land; I will give it to you as an inheritance, a land flowing with milk and honey." I am the Lord your God, who has set you apart from the nations. (vv. 22-24)

The Crossroads Principle simply stated is, "Am I to make a willful, knowledgeable and cognizant decision to live distinctly for God or just blend in to all facets of daily life?" Just as God challenged his people in the Old Testament, setting the tone for how the Israelites were to live a radical existence apart from the cultural norms of their day, so is God using that same principle to challenge his people today. Is it possible to make a willful, knowledgeable and cognizant decision to live counterculturally to the socially accepted norms of how to relate to, and build a bridge with, the GLBT community?

The wonderful part of the way that God allows us to live is that we can make an informed choice for ourselves. But that freedom can be scary. Many Christians are able to walk up to the edge of the cliff in their relationships with GLBT people. But when they see for themselves the vast uncertainty in relating meaningfully to them and the cost which such relationships may have, many just turn back and retreat to their own comfortable ways of living and believing.

This is to be an all or nothing decision both in life, and in building bridges with gays and lesbians—just as it was an all or nothing decision when the Israelites entered the Promised Land. To choose God and live set apart is to choose a difficult life. It's just so much easier to believe in God and blend in with everyone else, whether that's blending into everyday Christianity or mainstream society. But choose carefully because halfway is just not good enough.

Another way to conceptualize God's call at the crossroad is through a deliberate opting-out of mainstream norms. We all grasp the controversial nature of GLBT-Christian relations and the normal mode in which those relations are handled. But God is not for street brawls. He is not for arguments and debates. Our Lord is about a sacrifice paid that freely allows his followers to unconditionally love. Christians are held to God's countercultural standard that focuses solely on him and his worth in our daily lives, and how that relates to others. It is the Christian community's charge then to live in such a way throughout the world—and also within the GLBT community.

According to John Stott, the countercultural command God gave to the Israelites here in Leviticus is also paralleled throughout Scripture in Ezekiel 11:12, Matthew 6:8 and Romans 12:2. The New Testament goes into even more depth paralleling this command in Matthew 5:13-16, Luke 22:24-26, Ephesians 4:17-24 and 1 Peter 2:11-12. All of these passages highlight and affirm God's desire for us to live as intended through the Crossroads Principle: the radical call to the countercultural living that the Father expects from his followers.[6]

Those followers also include gays and lesbians. And just as we are to live set apart through our belief, so is God calling the GLBT community to make a willful, knowledgeable and cognizant decision to live distinctly in all facets of daily life. This countercultural decision starts by opting out of the relational norms of arguing, debating and fighting against conservatives. I have earnestly urged the Christian community throughout this book to do the same, but I recognize that a bridge cannot be built from only one side. Therefore the more the body of Christ can humbly assist the GLBT community to realize such eternal principles as the Crossroads one—that their identity is rooted in Christ first and foremost, and that they're able to live counterculturally as a distinct believer who doesn't have to conform to the accepted means of mainstream—the more all of God's children can collectively move toward a more intimate relationship with him.

ONENESS PRINCIPLE: ROMANS 1:26-27

Once a person has made a cognizant decision to either fully live for God, or not for God, they have decided what a relationship with God means to their lives and how that will influence their future path. From that choice comes the Oneness Principle: "Anything that positively or negatively affects an individual's one-on-one relationship with the Lord—or, for that matter, a person's formal divorce from the Lord."

Each of the aforementioned relational results between God and man fall under the rubric of the Oneness Principle, which follows naturally after the Crossroads Principle and its willful, knowledgeable and cognizant decision made about God. The broader passage of Romans 1:18-32 speaks to such a decision to not live for God. Specifically Romans 1:26-27 relates how homosexuality in a Roman cultural context can be a part of that progression:

> Because of this, God gave them over to shameful lusts. Even their women exchanged natural relations for unnatural ones. In the same way the men also abandoned natural relations with women and were inflamed with lust for one another. Men committed indecent acts with other men, and received in themselves the due penalty for their perversion.

Pro-gay theologians suggest that Paul is speaking specifically to the Greco-Roman practice of pederasty, broadly defined as the love of boys, which in those days was an ingrained part of Roman culture. There were four main types of pederasty in ancient Rome according to Robin Scroggs in *The New Testament and Homosexuality*: adult male "mentors" and educators who interacted sexually with their young male pupils, older men accumulating younger male house attendants who were used as sex slaves, older men forcing younger boys into same-sex prostitution for profit, and a career choice as a castrated male prostitute.[7]

Pederasty was so common that the Roman government taxed same-sex prostitution, with the money going directly to the emperor, and they also required a "holiday"—one day off per year—for boy prostitutes. No stigma whatsoever resulted from such prostitution, so the Romans freely prostituted anyone from slaves to family members, according to John Boswell in *Christianity, Social Tolerance, and Homosexuality*.[8] The conservative Christian community recognizes pederasty as common in the ancient Roman and Greek cultures but argues nevertheless that Paul is speaking not just to pederasty but also to consensual same-sex adult sexual relationships. Unfortunately for the current debate, no one is able to go back and ask Paul exactly what he was speaking about.

The Oneness Principle thus moves beyond the particulars by looking at the broader passage of verses 18-32. In addition to taking its readers step by step through the first two principles, this passage is also structurally similar to the passages in Leviticus—introduction (Mind-Frame-Shift Principle, vv. 18-21), body (Crossroads Principle, vv. 22-23) and conclusion (Oneness Principle, vv. 24-32).

In verses 18-21 Paul reminds believers that God plainly makes himself known to everyone; it's then a matter of shifting their mind frame to be able to fully accept that knowledge and be able to move forward focused on God. The Roman citizens Paul describes in this passage knew God and reached their crossroads, and a willful, knowledgeable and cognizant choice was made "not for God." The Romans' lie in verse 25 was their pagan worship of gods—idols made in the form of men and women, birds, animals and reptiles. The cause-and-effect relationship between their crossroads decision and subsequent integration of that decision led to the conclusion in verses 24-32.

I hear from many nonreligious gays and lesbians that these specific verses in 24-32 are proof that God hates GLBT people because he decided to "give them over." Their thinking is, *If God gave us over, why should we fight so hard to try to believe?*

But Paul writes "God gave them over" as a consequence of people's rejection of God. God did not give them over *because* they had same-sex attraction any more than he gave them over because they had been greedy, deceitful, malicious, gossipy, slanderous, insolent, arrogant, boastful or disobedient to their parents. If that was the case then he'd give up on everyone.

God doesn't give up. He was rejected, and rejection removes the Spirit's restraint and allows sin through one's unbelief to take its course. This pattern is paralleled in God's relationship with Israel in 2 Kings 17:7-23 when he removed himself from them after their continued practice of idol worship and sorcery.

There have been some biblical scholars who look at Romans 1:18-32 as one of the most negative portraits of humanity without God imaginable. If that's so, wouldn't the opposite of 18-32 be one of the most positive portrayals of life lived for God? A pastor friend of mine recently rewrote Romans 1:24-32 from the perspective of this ultimate positive:

> Therefore, God gave them over in their hearts to self-control and purity, that their bodies might be honored among them. For they kept and cherished the truth of God and worshiped and served the Creator, who is blessed forever, rather than the creature. Amen.
>
> For this reason God gave them over to pure and wholesome lives, lived with carefree ease even in the most intimate relations so that all received in their own person the due reward of their fidelity.

And just as they saw fit to acknowledge God in all things, God gave them over to a sound mind, to do those things which are proper, being filled with all righteousness, goodness, generosity, kindness; full of selflessness, life, healing, openness, kindliness; they are gentle in speech, always building others up, lovers of God, respectful, humble, self-effacing, inventors of good, obedient to parents, understanding, trustworthy, loving, merciful; and as they know the ordinance of God, that those who practice such things are possessors of life, they do the same, and give hearty approval to those who do like-wise.

Imagine what life could be like for those who, when facing the fork in the road, chose to believe in God and live out his revolutionary ways. Because of that choice the Oneness Principle, then, will fill the believer's life with all God intended for *all* his children.

What about GLBT-Christian relations in this context? Romans 1:18-32 draws on the Christian community's responsibility to learn about gays and lesbians and their firsthand thoughts, feelings and religious belief systems to translate an already existing knowledge of God into a personal, close, intimate, one-on-one relationship with him. As gays and lesbians choose for God, they begin the process of integrating their faith with a daily life that is permeated by God. God meets them, speaks to them and hears them, personally and individually telling each of his beloved children what he feels is best for their life.

As Paul so eloquently described in Romans 1, it is virtually impossible to accomplish any of those optimal ideals after a knowledgeable decision has been made not for God. Therefore the Christian community is responsible to do everything they possibly can to allow for a clear path to be made to God so that his full encompassing being will be able to work throughout all of our lives together.

THE GREAT CHRISTIAN DEBATE:
1 CORINTHIANS 6:9-11

At what point does a Christian release responsibility for someone else's life? This is the crux of the question at the heart of the fourth principle: the Great Christian Debate. It comes from 1 Corinthians 6:9-11:

> Do you not know that the wicked will not inherit the kingdom of God? Do not be deceived: Neither the sexually immoral nor idolaters nor adulterers nor male prostitutes nor homosexual offenders nor thieves nor the greedy nor drunkards nor slanderers nor swindlers will inherit the kingdom of God. And that is what some of you were. But you were washed, you were sanctified, you were justified in the name of the Lord Jesus Christ and by the Spirit of our God.

The vice list in this passage makes a blanket indictment of the people it lists as wicked and thus not qualified to enter the kingdom. Gays and lesbians read this passage and feel that Paul is telling them that all hope to inherit the kingdom of God is lost. Is it any wonder then why pro-gay theologians and gay Christians fight so hard to prove that Paul was actually talking about pederasty and not committed monogamous same-sex relationships? But there is much more going on in this passage.

Corinth was founded in A.D. 44 after Julius Caesar decided to make it a Roman colony. Because of its location to the Mediterranean many wealthy Grecian businessmen settled at Corinth's bustling ports. It quickly became a vital cog of culture and trade as a major urban center in the Roman Empire.

In A.D. 50 Paul founded the Corinthian church on his second missionary journey, and lived there a total of five years between two different trips—the longest amount of time, according to Geoffrey Bromiley, that Paul lived in any city during his ministry.[9] With such an extensive stay, Paul knew exactly what he was dealing with as he wrote his letters—he knew the people, the culture and the religion.

As was the case with most pagan-dominated cultures of the ancient times, Corinth relied heavily on an ancient Greek philosophy that was obsessed with beauty and pleasurable sexual expression, as well as a belief that the body was inherently evil. It was for these reasons that Paul had to remind the Corinthians that the body is a temple of the Holy Spirit (1 Cor 6:19). It was also these former pagans who had become believers that were now leading the Corinthian church. This text then must be taken as an attempt by Paul to reach out and shine God's light into the lives of these relatively new believers regarding their life in Christ—in stark contrast to their ingrained, old way of living.

The goal of this letter was to bring the Corinthian church back to its founding Christian principles and practices. Paul had gotten word that the surrounding Greco-Roman pagan culture had begun to dominate the theological, social and intellectual beliefs of those in the church. Christian scholar John MacArthur calls the temple prostitution, street prostitution and promiscuous sex that were all common practices Paul acknowledged in his letter (1 Cor 6:12-13) "Corinthianizing practices." The Corinthian church, meant to be a local expression of the kingdom of God, was in danger of becoming Corinthianized, and Paul wanted to stop them before it was too late. Paul deeply cared for the Corinthians' spiritual well being, just as the body of Christ should today for gays and lesbians.

The Christian-GLBT conversation related to verses 9-11 is focused on two Greek words in verse 9: *malakoi* (defined as "male prostitute") and *arsenokoitēs* (defined as "homosexual offender"). Only in the Bible—nowhere else in ancient literature—do we see the word *arsenokoitēs,* and only in the Bible do we see *malakoi* and *arsenokoitēs* used in combination with each other. Many believe that Paul coined both of these usages. In any case, there is an important point about this vice list that gets overlooked when we focus in too tightly on the disputed words.

The broader issue that the ten vices raise is the consideration of who is "wicked" and why they can't inherit the kingdom of God.

Paul gives us a unique insight into these questions. The Greek word
for "wicked" is *adikos*, and it is traditionally translated as "unjust,
unrighteous, unbeliever; wicked person." By understanding Paul's
filtration we start to get a clearer picture of what this vice list means.
By all accounts of "wicked" then, no unjust, unrighteous, unbeliev-
ing pagan can inherit the kingdom of God no matter who they are.
Paul's discernment of inheritance does not stand alone, as it's also
in harmony with Jesus' response to Nicodemus about who can enter
the kingdom of God (Jn 3:5-8): only by being born of the Spirit will
one enter, for only Spirit gives birth to spirit. Within the context of
that being "what some of [them] were" in both faith and deed, potential inheritance of the kingdom of God is birthed out of belief, first
and foremost.

A GLBT person has no hope of inheriting the kingdom of God
without belief. Yet if a belief exists, the starting point has been
reached and the Holy Spirit will then call people to tangibly express
that belief in Jesus Christ within their everyday lives. It's that simple. Paul is trying to remind the Corinthians of that simple faith as
he concludes this passage with a strong emphasis on such a point—
explaining the reason for the letter in the first place: "You were
washed, you were sanctified, you were justified in the name of the
Lord Jesus Christ and by the Spirit of our God."

A thorough understanding of "washed, sanctified and justified"
helps us understand the Great Christian Debate: where our responsibility for one another's eternal life ends. By conservative lexical
and biblical definitions, being washed is understood as a freedom
of sin through a commitment to God. Sanctification is defined as
the route by which the person's belief takes them from a state of
corruption to a state of holiness. And justification is defined as a
state of righteousness, made available through faith in Christ. A
literal reading of verse 11 brings more clarity to Paul's main point:

> Yes, pagan and unbelieving in faith and deed is what some of
> you were. But you have been washed by submitting yourselves
> for washing through the freedom of your sins through your

commitment to God. You have been sanctified by the purity from being set free from the guilt of your sins in which you have been taken from a state of corruption to a state of holiness. And you have been justified, showing yourselves righteous in your wish to be considered so, because in the name of the Lord Jesus Christ and by the Spirit of our God, all of these things have been made available to you through your faith in Christ.

Here Paul brings his message home to the pagan-dominated Corinthian Christian church: we inherit the kingdom of God through three simple steps in faith. Throughout antiquity leaders of the church were usually higher-status members of society. As was the ill-fated case with the leaders in Corinth, they readily brought with them the sexualized philosophical norms of the day. This understanding, and Paul's reminder, makes sense of the remainder of verses 12-20.

But with all of the Corinthian church's problems, filled with people who were seemingly not making any "progress," Paul knew he couldn't keep going back to fix everything. He couldn't just hop on a plane and be in Corinth later that evening to personally sort out the issues. A letter was his best means. Paul was conscious of the harsh realization in play: at what point do the Corinthians take what he taught and wrote, and stand on their own two feet? Just the same, at what point do Christians release control and the full responsibility to save someone else's life for what we might think is best?

When it comes to Christians' relationship with gays and lesbians, the Great Christian Debate encourages us to plant, water and feed, also recognizing that at some point GLBT people have to stand on their own in faith, with God. You can live a life in relationship with gays and lesbians that clearly defines a simple faith to inheriting the kingdom of God, and yet you can't make anyone do anything they are not themselves convinced about. When do gays and lesbians have the right to be their own person in Christ, regardless of whether a Christian agrees with their conclusion—whether that conclusion is to be a gay Christian or nonbeliever?

Love and grace still must persist even when two people, or two believers, don't see eye to eye. And yet releasing responsibility does not mean giving up, letting go or walking away! To release responsibility for a person to God is to remain unconditionally there for them and always provide the unrestricted path to God in both faith and deeds, all the while trusting in God's ultimate power to continue to shape their journey of faith—just as Paul did with the Corinthian church.

THINK-BIG-PICTURE PRINCIPLE: 1 TIMOTHY 1:9-11

Living a life committed to the gospel is a sacrifice—a rough road to choose and a rough road to endure. The Think-Big-Picture Principle, our fifth and final principle, prompts us to trust God by standing firm and persevering in our calling because each person has until their very last breath to accomplish what God has set forth for their life. This principle is pulled from the book of 1 Timothy and relates specifically to chapter 1, verses 9-11.

> We also know that law is made not for the righteous but for lawbreakers and rebels, the ungodly and sinful, the unholy and irreligious; for those who kill their fathers or mothers, for murderers, for adulterers and perverts, for slave traders and liars and perjurers—and for whatever else is contrary to the sound doctrine that conforms to the glorious gospel of the blessed God, which he entrusted to me.

Verse 10 includes the Greek word *arsenokoitēs,* translated here as "perverts" rather than "homosexual offender" as in 1 Corinthians 6. As such, this passage is included in biblical discussions about homosexuality—and of course is not without controversy. But as we've established, the responsible approach to this controversial passage is not starting with the word but the big picture.

Things that are time-sensitive expire. Due to some "expiration issues" with food growing up, my wife vigilantly watches the dates on grocery products so that neither of us will ever eat or drink anything that is even remotely close to expiring. Food expires. Batteries expire. Hours in a day expire. Reorientation programs eventually run out of steps and therefore expire as well. God doesn't expire, however; he continues to pursue people. And so any effort to pursue people on God's behalf needs to forgo expiration dates as well.

This letter to Timothy, along with 2 Timothy and the book of Titus, are called the Pastoral Epistles because they offer insight from an outstanding pastor on how to properly shepherd people in faith, love, time and patience. Paul wanted Timothy and Titus to reflect these qualities at their core. By the time 1 Timothy was written (around A.D. 62), Paul was in Macedonia, advanced in age and conscious that his time on earth would soon end. For years he had been on a tear from city to city, zealously pursuing the Lord and spreading the good news. Paul eventually recognized that his blazing trail also left some burned areas. I don't know one person at the end of their life who didn't take a moment to look back and reflect to see if it was all worthwhile—asking themselves what legacy they left, and what impact they made. Those same questions were a driving force behind Paul's letters.

I love the movie *Mr. & Mrs. Smith* starring Brad Pitt and Angelina Jolie. I remember sitting in the theater watching it for the first time, gripped by its action, when a scene toward the end provoked my mind to this exact passage of Scripture in 1 Timothy. Pitt, a professional hit man, is driving in a stolen car after a failed attempt on his life by his wife, Jolie, who is also a professional assassin. They've only just discovered one another's hidden professions. Pitt calls Jolie and asks a series of questions about love and the beginning of their relationship because he's trying to figure out if their marriage was just a cover for Jolie to steal information. Pitt's questioning flusters her because she actually did love him, even though it is now her "job" to kill him. She asks why, after all this time, he's now questioning their relationship. Pitt responds, "When the end is near, you start to reflect on the beginning."

As soon as I heard that I realized what Paul was thinking as he
wrote this letter to Timothy. Paul was not only a mentor to Timothy,
but also a father figure. Many scholars believe that Paul was directly
responsible for Timothy's conversion to the faith (Acts 16:1; 1 Cor
4:16; 1 Tim 1:2), which is why Timothy so willfully traveled with
Paul and earnestly looked to him as his spiritual father.[10] Timothy
had remained in Ephesus to lead the church while his mentor continued on his ordained missionary journeys. Over time many difficulties cropped up in the Ephesian church, and upon hearing Timothy's situation Paul began to realize that these were the same types
of difficulties he had been encountering throughout the many years
of his traveling ministry. This letter to Timothy is thus comparable
to the last words written by an elderly loved one summarizing the
truths and lessons learned throughout their lifetime. Paul didn't
want history to repeat itself, and he was passing on all that he
learned from his difficult experiences, specifically in Corinth, so
that none of the same things would happen to Timothy's church in
Ephesus (1 Tim 1:3-4). This is also the reason why the vice lists in
1 Corinthians 6 and 1 Timothy 1 are so similar.

There is not a quick fix to anything. Nothing is without drama.
Unconditional commitment with no expiration date only has one
rationale: God commands us to build sustainable and relational
bridges for people to encounter his love and establish his kingdom
together. And that is what Paul is saying in his final set of letters to
his young, exuberant and yet timid disciple: stay, be faithful, perse-
vere and plan for the long term by thinking about the bigger picture
of what a faithful commitment will ultimately do for the kingdom.

We'll never know what will be accomplished in a person's life
until their final breath is literally taken. Everyone—gay or straight,
Paul or Timothy, the people of Corinth or the people of Ephesus—
has until the moment of their death to accomplish what God has set
forth for their life. That reality was never more apparent than when
Jesus spoke with two convicted robbers nailed to crosses on his
right and left sides (Lk 23:32-43). Both robbers knew they were re-

ceiving the right ruling for their actions. Using their last breath one accused Jesus and one embraced Jesus. And one of Jesus' last acts before his death was to usher that embracing convicted robber into paradise. At the moment of his own death Jesus never gave up hope for another's life—even for a criminal at the end of his life.

God's plan is always greater than our own. We don't know when, where, why or how any of it will get done. But as long as the door is open and there is still a breath, the opportunity to strive one more time toward God is there as well. Since I started The Marin Foundation, Paul's main theme in 1 Timothy has come to life. There have been some particular moments when I was ready to walk away, convinced that I had done everything I possibly could to see this thing through. Every time that thought occurs, though, my belly burns with "what ifs" as my mind can't escape thinking in terms of the unknowns that lay ahead in the bigger picture.

What if through The Marin Foundation more churches become sensitive to the challenges of seeking God within the gay community by moving past their prejudices? What if those churches then begin to build bridges in their own local GLBT community?

What if through The Marin Foundation some GLBT people learn that God loves them unconditionally and has a better life and eternity in mind for them? What if they move beyond their prejudices about Christians and discover the joy of authentic Christian community?

What if through The Marin Foundation the conversation changes between the Christian community and the GLBT community? What if there's a revival of faith among GLBT people and a church ready to help them navigate their new relationships with God in Christ?

I could have never guessed what God had in store for this one-time Bible-banging homophobe. And neither can I now guess what God has in store for GLBT-Christian relations. The Lord was faithful enough, and loving enough, gave time enough and was patient enough to accomplish all he had planned with Paul, a man who fought against and defamed Christianity. I can only wonder if there is a correlation there somewhere between God's patience with Paul, Paul's patience with the people he brought the gospel to, Paul's lesson to Timothy, and the patience God is calling his church toward today with gays and lesbians.

THE BIG 5 PRINCIPLES TAKEN TOGETHER

To elevate does not mean to ignore. Rather, elevating the conversation between the GLBT and Christian communities means making a choice to stop the fight, understanding the differences that tear the GLBT and Christian communities apart and then seeking God and his eternal principles that bridge these two groups of people. God's intentions are clearly revealed within the passages in Scripture that speak to homosexuality:

1. to shift each person's mind frame away from the things that bind our yearning for anything else but God

2. to bring each person to their own crossroads of belief where they make a choice to live distinctly for him or not

3. to recognize from that choice what positively or negatively affects an individual's oneness with the Lord

4. to know when to release control of someone else's life

5. to keep open a path for God to accomplish his will for a person's life, even until their last breath

These Big 5 Principles can be seen in the traditional battleground passages that have torn the GLBT and Christian communities apart—proof that God has not finished with any of us yet. The Big 5 gives us all a common ground and a common purpose to continue to strive toward Jesus by hermeneutically elevating a conversation that has caused so much hurt and pain on both sides. The gates of the kingdom of heaven are wide open as we have been charged with the task of building that sustainable bridge where it has never been built before.

The work of The Marin Foundation among the GLBT community

is based on sixteen commitments to a peaceful, productive and sustainable relationship that makes a significant impact for the kingdom. They are not sixteen steps, nor are they a program. They are a way of life that breaks down into three sections—the foundational base, the approach and the implementation. For the remainder of the book we'll look at how this unique bridge gets built, plank by plank.

8

Laying the Foundation

Commitment, Boldness and the Big 5

Over the years I have had the privilege to learn from Christian HIV/AIDS physician Becky Kuhn of Global Lifeworks (www.global lifeworks.org)—an organization dedicated to education and collaboration for a healthier HIV/AIDS community. Dr. Becky works in the United States with infected homeless people with no insurance, and with churches about how to get involved with this pandemic. Internationally her organization has assisted in planting an HIV/AIDS clinic for people who live in an impoverished area in South Africa and provided HIV/AIDS education in India and South Africa.

Dr. Becky has come to realize a pattern not only with her HIV/AIDS patients but also with the gay and lesbian people she knows and loves. No matter where in the world she finds herself, the one common thread between everyone is that they only ask two things of her:

- "Please don't lie to me."
- "Please don't leave me."

And she doesn't do either of those things, all in the name of our Father. The first time I heard her say those words was at a training she gave at a church in Grand Rapids, Michigan. I was struck with her sincerity and the gentleness in how she related that simple, yet agonizing reality of what too many people have had to go through when it comes to our actions, and reactions, as believing Christians. It broke my heart to hear her patients' two requests because I have been confronted with too many people who have suffered from a Christian commitment gone wrong. But what broke my heart even more was the realization that everyone in that audience needed to hear those words.

Just think of how many gay and lesbian people in Grand Rapids have been lied to or left by a member of that congregation. Don't get me wrong—I am not pinpointing either that church or the city of Grand Rapids. I can easily substitute any church or city, including my own, and the example would still be as relevant. Just don't lie to me, and don't leave me—words the Christian community must take seriously as we recognize our command to build a bridge.

COMMITMENT 1: COMMITMENT

A young and successful Christian businessman I know has all the money he needs and all the looks to back up his skyrocketing career. He has a girlfriend whom he's attracted to but sexually chaste with. However, he has one small secret that he has been keeping from everyone: the anonymous sex with other males behind his girlfriend's back.

Over the past year he has gone to the altar at his church on three separate occasions during the service to ask his pastor for help. Each time the pastor promised to follow up with him and never did, leaving him more depressed as he continued to sink further and further away. It took a lot of guts for him to turn to The Marin Foundation and tell me his story after how he had been forgotten. When I told him that I wasn't going to leave, that I would follow through and that I would help him however he needs to be helped, tears started to fill his eyes and he smiled.

I thought he was happy because he finally found someone he could trust. Boy was I wrong. He looked at me and said, "Do you know how many times I've heard that before? I'm only telling you all of this so my conscience is clear. God knows how many of his people have given up, or not tried at all." With that he paid for his meal, got up, thanked me for my time and promptly left.

What just happened? I had never had anything like that happen to me before, and I was really mad. Who was that guy to think I was like all the others? He just used me as a means to feel better, like I was some type of confessional he needed to justify what he was doing emotionally and physically to himself and his girlfriend. I just wasted an hour of my time. I got up and headed out.

No more than two steps out the door I realized something myself: *Who was I to think that he would believe me when I said those things?* That exact situation has happened to him three other times that I know of, by a person whom he trusted for help. He didn't want words, he didn't want a feeling; he wanted me to follow through.

And so that is what I did. As soon as I got back to my desk I emailed and called him to let him know I meant what I said. It's been almost a year since that first encounter and he's on a tough journey right now. But it's sure a lot easier when you know someone isn't going to give up on you.

When it comes to same-sex sexual attractions and behaviors, Christians just give up too easily. Therefore above anything else when it comes to the GLBT community, the most important thing Christians can do is make a commitment for the long haul. Without a genuine commitment on the Christian's part there can be, and will be, nothing other than meaningless talk and niceties. I hear the same thing again and again from GLBT youth and adults: "I would have rather had Christians never enter my life than to continue entering in and then leaving. It does more harm than good."

Just read that statement again. Only through a real commitment without knowing what's going to happen can believers take the first step to restoring a bridge with the GLBT community.

When I first immersed myself in the GLBT community I had no idea what I was doing or what good could ever come out of my decision. The only thing I did know was that I was in it for the long haul, because in my mind, there was no turning back. God will always be faithful to our commitments if we can only be faithful to our own.

I know that committing to something that most of us know nothing about is not easy. When we are walking into an unknown we need assurance that there is hope to one day pull us through the times that we know will come, the times we know we can't handle. God will fill in those gaps if only we solidify in ourselves the commitment to stay. Remember that God gives the growth, Jesus causes us to stand, and it is our job to obey. After we have committed ourselves, all we can do is stand faithfully.

COMMITMENT 2: BOLDNESS

Boldness is a matter of intentionality. Christians must take the lead in stopping pointless arguments and debates, confronting sexuality's infinite continuum, and refusing to use closed-ended questions.

The Marin Foundation's slogan is "Be Bold." Yet when most people look at that they think of being bold in the traditional understanding— "if I'm bold, then I'm in your face." I believe that being bold involves a bigger vision, having nothing to do with antagonistic confrontation.

Each year Chicago's Gay Pride Parade occurs in my neighborhood. The city's second largest parade, with over 250 floats and more than 400,000 people in attendance, it runs eight blocks up and down the main street in Boystown. With so many GLBT people condensed in such a tight location, especially when there might be quite a bit of alcohol consumption involved, Chicago's Gay Pride Parade is not the best time or place to make a religious statement against same-sex sexual behavior. But people do it anyway.

A very traditional conservative church is located right on the main strip of road that the parade goes through. This church has a large building and a massive gated parking lot in front of its doors. It's been there since the mid-1900s; Boystown has actually built itself around the church. Each year during the Gay Pride Parade members from that church stand inside their gated parking lot (some of them do venture outside) and hold up gigantic signs connected to tall poles so everyone can read them, with such classic phrases as "Homosexuality is a sin!" "Repent or go to hell!" My favorite? "God loves you."

I've always found it interesting that Christians expect a nice, cordial response to the words on the signs. Or even better, they expect GLBT people to read that God loves them alongside words of condemnation, and automatically realize their "error" in being gay and decide to listen to those messages—rather than listening to the numerous floats in the parade from gay affirming churches. Why would they need to bother listening to the Bible-bangers? They wouldn't; and believe me, they don't.

I once asked representatives from that church why they do what they do. Their answer was that they believed there needed to be a voice of opposition, so the gay community knows that not everyone agrees with a pro-gay stance. The GLBT community already knows there is opposition to their life! They're not going to forget that there is a huge conservatively religious cross section of the population that doesn't think homosexuality is OK! That church now has police protection surrounding them each year during the parade.

The members of that church complain to media outlets about how they're treated by parade participants, and yet they keep holding up those signs year after year in the middle of this huge GLBT event in the third largest city in the country. What are they trying to accomplish other than to voice scorn for the GLBT community? Picketing and holding up signs is not being bold. It's rude, inconsiderate, dim-witted and wrong. Nothing positive can come out of such a thing.

Being bold for Scripture has nothing to do with pickets and signs. Biblical boldness is characterized by Paul's words in 1 Corinthians 9:20-22:

> To the Jews I became like a Jew, to win the Jews. To those under the law I became like one under the law (though I myself am not under the law), so as to win those under the law. To those not having the law I became like one not having the law (though

I am not free from God's law but am under Christ's law), so as to win those not having the law. To the weak I became weak, to win the weak. I have become all things to all men so that by all possible means I might save some.

I'm not sure how many GLBT people have come to know the Lord through the church's signs, but I do know that in the last couple of years almost a dozen people have started to attend Bible-believing churches. I know because each year people from The Marin Foundation plant ourselves right across the street from that church, and from early in the morning to well after the parade has finished we hang out and engage people in nonthreatening, peaceful and productive conversations. We don't try to argue or prove a point; we just want to represent Jesus, who we think would be productively immersed in the community.

In the Bible the word *bold* and its conjugations *boldly* and *boldness* appear twenty-four times. These words are used to describe four main constructs: boldness in action, belief, character and word. The common thread behind each of these uses is the theme of intentionality. Being bold in action, belief, character and word is not in many people's nature. For someone to step out and be bold is a commitment in and of itself to God's will. Yet the intentional boldness that I am talking about is the same countercultural boldness that Jesus reflected throughout his time on earth—one rooted in discipleship. It's easy to stand with a sign; it's difficult and bold to intentionally live life with another human to make a significant impact for the kingdom.

Jesus makes very clear his interpretation of discipleship. According to Charles Swindoll and Roy Zuck, there are eleven key elements to faithful, godly discipleship: deny yourself; take up your cross daily; keep on following Christ; submit all that life is for Christ's purpose; continue in Christ's Word; practice prayer according to Christ's teaching; abide in union with Christ; love Christ supremely; love one another; serve others; and make disciples.[1] Jesus' understanding of discipleship is not by means of evangelism but rather a way of life that is wholly committed to God. Through my lens about GLBT relations, this is why Jesus said, "If anyone comes to me and does not hate his father and mother, his wife and children, his brothers and sisters—yes, even his own life—he cannot be my disciple" (Lk 14:26); and "If you want to be perfect, go, sell your possessions. . . . Then come, follow me" (Mt 19:21). There is only one way to live boldy for Christ—to be *fully* sold out to his ways to follow and live a biblical boldness within the context of a bridge-building relationship.

COMMITMENT 3:
APPLYING THE MIND-FRAME-SHIFT PRINCIPLE

Every Christian has a relational stumbling block that hinders their ability to assist a GLBT person to move forward in their relationship with Christ. When my friends came out to me, the idea of them having sex with someone else of the same sex grossed me out. I felt ashamed and sick to my stomach every time I looked in their eyes because of the thoughts that perseverated in my head. Those images were putting a large chasm between me and them—I knew it and they knew it. The only thing that saved me in that situation was my friends coming to *me* to talk about God.

I recognize, though, that there are many Christians who don't have gay or lesbian friends who openly approach them about God. In order to counter this common situation Christians must get over their own stumbling blocks before any bridge building can occur. How does a person get past their stumbling blocks? The first things to understand are the paralyzers—those issues that you know will affect your capacity to build a bridge. As long as paralyzers exist, Christians will be too caught up focusing on the wrong topic. My paralyzer was "the act," while other people get tripped up over aspects of GLBT culture, "out and proud" social behavior or any number of varying inhibitors. Through experience, and a lot of help from many GLBT people who have humbly allowed me to figure these situations out with them, I have learned to "deparalyze" myself, my thoughts and my actions.

Christians need to face the reality that we are limited in our capacity to love, even in the midst of meaningful relationships. Just by being self-aware that potential paralyzers might one day surface will put your future efforts ahead of many others at the same point. It's perfectly acceptable, and *normal*, to recognize that some topics or constructs of truth within the GLBT life might be too much of a shock to your system—the causer of what paralyzes. With that recognition, it is important to immediately bring our stumbling blocks before God. This isn't a trite "Lord, change me." It is rather a serious self-exposure which deconstructs an old mind that stifles our ability to see God and the GLBT community clearly.

Last month I saw the movie *Evan Almighty* for the first time. Watching it for entertainment purposes, I never expected to find anything profound. Then in the middle of the movie I heard something that really challenged my theological understanding of the nontraditional ways of our Father. After Evan's wife and kids left him because they thought he was totally crazy for believing that "God told him to build an ark in the middle of Washington, D.C.," God appeared to Evan's wife and said,

> If someone prays for patience, do you think God gives them patience or does he give them the opportunity to be patient? If someone prays for courage, does he give them courage or does he give them opportunities to be courageous? If someone prayed for the family to be closer, do you think God zaps them with warm, fuzzy feelings, or does he give them opportunities to love each other?

This is the opportunity God has given Christians with the GLBT community. What has always stopped Christians in the past is an opportunity to overcome, and find the answers to our prayers—how can the body of Christ ever know how to build a bridge with gays and lesbians? Christians, then, must admit our paralyzers to our gay and lesbian friends. Yes, it's totally frightening. Yes, you're scared that such an admission will give them reason to cast you off.

But to come before the GLBT community, having to humbly lower ourselves and ask for their patience and understanding as we struggle to work through all of these new dynamics, we might—just for a fading second—enter into what it means to live in the GLBT-Christian tension from their perspective. In doing so, we have truly learned to shift our mind frame.

COMMITMENT 4:
APPLYING THE CROSSROADS PRINCIPLE

The Crossroads Principle doesn't just apply to our relationship with God. It also applies to our relationships with the people God has brought us into contact with. Will we make a willful, knowledgeable and cognizant decision to live differently regarding the gay and lesbian community, or will we just stay the same? The apostle Peter details the countercultural life on the far side of this crossroads in 1 Peter 4:1-11.

> Therefore, since Christ suffered in his body, arm yourselves also with the same attitude, because he who has suffered in his body is done with sin. As a result, he does not live the rest of his earthly life for evil human desires, but rather for the will of God. . . . They think it strange that you do not plunge with them into the same flood of dissipation, and they heap abuse on you. But they will have to give account to him who is ready to judge the living and the dead. . . . Therefore be clear minded and self-controlled so that you can pray. Above all, love each other deeply, because love covers over a multitude of sins. Offer hospitality to one another without grumbling. Each one should use whatever gift he has received to serve others, faithfully administering God's grace in its various forms. If anyone speaks, he should do it as one speaking the very words of God. If anyone serves, he should do it with the strength God provides, so that in all things God may be praised through Jesus Christ. To him be the glory and the power for ever and ever. Amen.

Here Peter is referring to the spiritual bond created by a life chosen for God and his ways, in direct opposition to the culturally accepted multitude of diverse interests that pull believers in all different directions.[2] This is why Jesus said in Matthew 7:13-14, "Wide is
the gate and broad is the road that leads to destruction, and many
enter through it. But small is the gate and narrow the road that leads
to life, and only a few find it."

Throughout the entirety of Scripture the Father is calling his
sheep to realize this radical way of life. But still few are able to find
it—to leave the judging to God, to leave the convicting to the Holy
Spirit and to embrace the orientation of love. To worship with, go to
church with, explore difficult questions with, be real with and be
intentionally committed to live life with people who are honestly
open to the call of God on their life. To hang out with people when
they need someone, to offer patience when people need time and
freedom to discover who they are in God. Above all, to praise the
Lord for such wonderfully unique opportunities to love.

These choices are not about gays and lesbians, they're about us.
To be different with a purpose is closer to the Father's original intent for his people, and it all starts with just one willful, knowledgeable and cognizant choice.

COMMITMENT 5: APPLYING THE ONENESS PRINCIPLE

When a decision for God is made, the next major movement of
growth is communication. The ultimate ideal for the Oneness Principle is that gays and lesbians would one day be able to confidently
say that the Lord talks to them and they hear him, and that they talk
to the Lord and he hears them.

Communication in the Spirit breeds eternal understanding and
righteous living. But the overwhelming pressure to see a conclusion
one way or the other inhibits this work of the Spirit. As Christians,
our job is not to coerce or pressure anyone, by fear or force of logic.
We can only take care of what we can control, and it's impossible to
control another human being's will and motivation. No matter how

much we might want something for a GLBT person, their convictions and beliefs are ultimately up to them.

I originally met Karen through a friend of a friend while I was still in college. She was in her mid-twenties and had recently gotten herself into trouble. A couple of DUIs and a few one-night stands with random women will get even the most avowed atheistic lesbian wondering what's going on. She knew I was a straight Christian because our mutual friend had told her as much. When we met for the first time the first words out of her mouth were, "I know what you believe. Don't try to convince me of anything."

I know there are a lot of people who dread those words. But I'm actually very thankful for them because I know the other person's expectations of the relationship from the start. The more we talked and the more she got to know me, the more she opened up about her life and belief, or lack thereof. She felt God had left her hanging out to dry on multiple occasions when she needed him the most.

Six years went by. Throughout that time we continued to talk and carry on our relationship. She would ask to come to church with me here and there, attend a Bible study here or there, or ask me a random question about God here or there. We would talk, she would thank me for my responses, and then never mention whatever issue we spoke about again.

This repeating pattern definitely got discouraging after the first couple of years of the same scenarios. But then I realized, *If not me, then who would she turn to with all these things?* I started to look at each moment with her as a rare blessing rather than a burden. Those thoughts not only eased my frustration but released me from the bitter feeling that I was doing all of these things just to say I did them.

After the sixth year my heart ached to see her release control of her life. I had never met anyone who fought so hard to keep everything in line. But I continued to respect the one rule of trust that she had asked me to keep from the very beginning. Then late one night she got home from her waitressing job and called me to tell me that she was tired of her life, and the only solution she could come up with was to try "the Jesus thing." She wanted to go to bed but promised to call me the following day so we could get together and talk more.

I woke up that next morning with anticipation for her call and our pending conversation. The day flew by, and no call ever came. I figured she was tired and we'd talk the following day, but the same thing happened. The day after that, it happened again. I was starting to wonder what was going on, so I called her. The phone rang once and an automated message came on saying that her number had been disconnected. I called our mutual friend and she called her as well, but got the same response. I called her work and they said she quit two nights earlier. I checked my email—nothing. She had always been very reserved and shy, but this was unlike her; she was always very respectful of her commitments and other people's time. I didn't know what else to do and so I started checking the obituaries, just in case. Nothing there either.

A week later I opened my inbox and saw her name. I opened the email with much trepidation as I had no idea what she was going to say. As I read it, it crippled me word by word:

Hi Andrew,

Thanks for everything. Thanks for being my friend. Thanks for talking and listening. Thanks for not judging me, that's never happened before outside of lesbians. I'm sorry I left how I did. I had to. I got too close. I got too scared. You know that I've been on my own for so long. The thought of you and [our mutual friend's name] was too much. I got a new number and this is the last email I'm sending from this account. I'm going to get a new one of those as well. But just know that all you did for me, I'll never forget any of it. Maybe one day God will let me know he's there. I know you're there, and you seem to know he's there. But I just can't; even though I think I could even admit that he is there. Anyway, maybe our paths will cross again.

I tried emailing her back but she indeed closed her account. I cried for about an hour. That's all I could muster at that point. Neither I nor our mutual friend had any way of getting hold of her. I haven't heard from her since, and I'm not sure if I ever will. I tried to Google her name and see what I could find. But she's pretty good at disappearing when she wants to.

I wonder about her sometimes. I wonder where she is and how she's doing. I still pray that she's happy. I do know, though, that our Father knows where she is and what she's up to. And he loves her. The Lord brought us together for something more than I can wrap my mind around. Today I can only hope it was to lay the groundwork for some other work of God.

But why? Why so long, and why did I have to invest so much for so little? Then again, was it really that little? I have no idea what might ever come out of those six years. Maybe one day she'll read this book and see her email and give me a call just to let me know she's alive and well. Maybe not. Maybe it's too much for me to ask. Regardless, I have to be OK knowing that year in and year out I faithfully did everything I could to make a significant impact for the kingdom in her life, cherishing every moment I spent sharing space with her. Shortly after I got that final email I read Ezekiel 33:2-6.

> When I bring the sword against a land, and the people of the land choose one of their men and make him their watchman, and he sees the sword coming against the land and blows the trumpet to warn the people, then if anyone hears the trumpet but does not take warning and the sword comes and takes his life, his blood will be on his own head. . . . But if the watchman sees the sword coming and does not blow the trumpet to warn the people and the sword comes and takes the life of one of them, that man will be taken away because of his sin, but I will hold the watchman accountable for his blood.

This passage is speaking to the faithfulness of a calling; Ezekiel was to be distinctly faithful to what God asked of him. In this situation he was assigned as the watchman to appeal to the Israelites to come back to God. For today's situation, Christians have been assigned to live out our faithfulness to God by reaching across and responding to all social and spiritual issues in such a way that follows God's ideal on how to live as a distinctive follower.

One of the most common misinterpretations of this passage, as it's applied to the GLBT community, is a justification to condemn and cast off gays and lesbians when they don't embrace the traditional ideal for human sexuality. "Since their blood is on their own head, then I, like Ezekiel, am off the hook." But the Lord is calling for so much more.

If the overarching principle of this passage is faithfulness, the bigger question is: how as Christians can we live faithfully to God's call in relation to the GLBT community? The answer is by incarnationally bridging the gap, focused on drawing all of God's children into a closer one-on-one relationship with him. Ezekiel could only do what was asked of him—to watch for God on behalf of his people, whether or not they listened. Therefore we must do the same: giving all of ourselves in honor of God's countercultural ways to reconciliation to draw all of his children closer to him—whether or not anyone listens to us either. What might happen in the end is not mutually exclusive to how Christians are to live faithfully, peacefully and productively alongside the GLBT community.

COMMITMENT 6:
APPLYING THE GREAT CHRISTIAN DEBATE

At what point does a Christian release responsibility for a gay or lesbian person's life and faith? Release responsibility? Don't continue to push sin and behavioral change in their faces? It's an interesting quandary with an even more provoking application. Releasing eternal responsibility while still loving in tangible and measurable expressions of unconditional behaviors actually gives GLBT people the room to live life, continuing to wrestle with issues that are beyond them, and us. The Great Christian Debate also releases the responsibility of thinking that it's a Christian's job to drag someone from gay to straight.

But as I am told living in the midst of this principle: "Gays and lesbians need to be told the truth. You're giving in. You're playing into their hands. You're giving up too easy. You're going down without a fight. They win when you're weak. You're not being a good Christian. You're a heretic. Why are you settling for what they want?" I hear that a lot. I have a hard time not questioning the integrity of those critics because every time I invite one of them to experience my life, they quickly decline.

Those who decline don't grasp that most people within the GLBT community who are threatened by traditional interpretations of the Bible as it pertains to homosexuality want nothing to do with it— and by extension, anyone who embraces it. How can Christians build a bridge in that circumstance? A piece of preliminary data from The Marin Foundation's national research study shows that 70 percent of GLBT people believe that the religious community is too forceful. Hence, continually attempting to convince a person that Christ is the ultimate Savior when they either don't want it or are not ready to receive it is the same as trying to rekill a dead horse.

This does not mean I am calling GLBT people spiritually dead; nor am I saying that believers are to just give up all hope. It does, however, mean that Christians are to find a different way to do everything they feel has been set forth for them by God. From my experience, that other way is to present themselves as an unforced open-ended option through sustainable relationships, and then accept whatever happens with their new understanding of what it means to love. A flesh-and-blood representation of Jesus Christ becomes Christianity's most effective form of building trust, forming that common ground in a belief that there is something more powerful out there petitioning our life.

Throughout my time immersed in the GLBT community I have experienced many lives and endings to stories that have ripped my heart out along the way, only to be renewed and refreshed as God's plan unfolded in a manner that left me dumbfounded. Even if our GLBT friends don't want to embrace what we have in Christ, they still know you're going to be there for them because you've *proven* so time and again. There is *always* an opportunity for spiritual growth through Jesus—whether or not you talk about it every time you're together. Christians must stop expecting change based on how hard one tries, and instead rely on and expect the Lord to move in people's lives—through his Spirit, on *his* timetable. No matter how much Christians want to speed up a process that they think is best, it just can't happen.

COMMITMENT 7:
APPLYING THE THINK-BIG-PICTURE PRINCIPLE

A few years ago I met a middle-aged gay man named Christopher. A friend of his had previously attended a workshop I gave and, from what I was told after the fact, strongly "encouraged" Christopher to take my organization's classes. The first class Christopher came to he beelined for the front row and sat in the first seat right in front of me. I was a little nervous about what could happen that afternoon because just looking at him I saw an incomparably smug sense of skepticism that completely soaked the room with its aroma. Up to that point my classes had generated only positive responses (and tear-filled conversations), but from the moment I began class that day Christopher jumped all over every word out of my mouth.

For two hours I felt like nothing more than a helpless deer in the headlights of a two-ton eighteen-wheeler about to run me over. And then for good measure after running me over, the semitruck backed over me and repeated the process a few hundred times, just in case I hadn't realized what hit me. To this day I'm not sure if he smelled the fear or if he was just that passionately hurt, doubtful or curious, but he let me have it either way. By the time my first ever onslaught in class was over I was completely frazzled.

I called my dad in tears thinking I was in way over my head. I felt like a fraud trying to accomplish the impossible, fooling myself into believing I could actually make a difference. I began to doubt the Lord's voice and everything I imagined The Marin Foundation to be. That entire next week I cowardly prayed Christopher wouldn't come back. My spirit was so fragile; I knew I didn't have all of the answers. I knew I couldn't heal his pain. I knew I didn't have the ability to withstand the raw emotions that exuded out of every pore of his body.

When the next class came around he showed up again. And the same thing happened. The only difference was, this time it wasn't just two hours, it was four. Beaten and self-conscious, I barely showed up for the following class. Guess who did as well? Christopher and all of his zealousness.

A friend of mine, Andrew Bronson, says that the word *interesting* isn't actually a word but a nonsensical description of the indescribable. My relationship with Christopher was *interesting*. After four long months of this pattern repeating itself I had not one shred of ability to withstand another class. I had been doubted, questioned, blamed, cursed at and antagonized hour after hour, week after week, month after month.

One day during the fifth month he came to class and did not make a peep. I thought to myself, *this is my only chance to actually set the tone and say something to him first before he starts up again.* Sarcastically I said, "What's wrong, are you not feeling OK today? Where are the comments?"

Christopher looked up at me, and as he unsuccessfully tried to hold back the tears, he began to tell his life story. It left me completely speechless to find out how his family had ruthlessly treated him throughout the years, all in the name of God. I did not know what to say to comfort him, encourage him or even give him any hope because I was professing my love for the same God that caused all of the terror in his life.

With each of his words I was embarrassed and extremely disappointed with myself for how I had thought about and treated him. I wasn't sure after that week if I would ever see him again, and for the first time I was actually hoping he would come back. Here is where the

Lord stepped in. Christopher did come back and even began giving me rides to and from class. After spending a lot of time talking in his van, I was finally able to work past my own self-doubt and work with what was a real and raw eagerness—the only way he knew how to truly learn and understand. About six months later Christopher ended up recommitting his life to Christ. A couple months after that he started to make appearances at the church I attended. Shortly after that he told me that some of his kids started having a faith in God as well.

I didn't understand what he meant by "his kids," because at that time I thought it was illegal for gay couples to adopt children. What I didn't know was that behind the scenes he and his partner of almost thirty years had willingly foster-parented sick, underprivileged and disadvantaged children from Mexico. They would bring these children to America and give them a life and an opportunity to succeed, away from the slums and poverty they once lived in. Christopher has four children—now adults, all straight. They each have families of their own now, along with a faith in God—because of Christopher.

Christopher has taught me so much about myself as a man in Christ, because through this experience I now understand what it's like to be able to stand in my faith and rest upon the realization that I actually don't really know that much. I thought I was doing something good with gays and lesbians; Christopher forced God's kingdom on my life by showing me all my incompleteness.

I've never met a more humble man than Christopher. I asked him if I could write about his life and my personal experience, and he wondered out loud, "My life isn't special. I don't know why you'd want to talk about me. I'm just like everyone else." But in my life, and now the lives of those who hear his story, Christopher has lived out the Think-Big-Picture Principle. If, at any time in the first *four* exasperating months, I had showed him the door because I was tired of responding, tired of doubting myself, tired of being discouraged, tired of my embarrassment and tired of constantly being on the defensive, who knows if he or his large family would have ever come to know the Lord.

Here now is that place of Martin Luther King Jr.'s constructive, nonviolent tension that the Christian community gets to grow within: Is Christopher's eternal legacy based on his sexuality? Or, is Christopher's eternal legacy directly correlated to what he did for his family, and his family's family, for generations to come?

I can't give the final answers to those questions; only God can. But what I do know is what I've seen with my own eyes. Confront yourself face to face with God through Christopher's story the next time you find yourself struggling with the difficulty that comes with attempting to build a bridge to someone who, as I perceived, was the most out and proud, militant GLBT person I had ever met. Are you just talking to someone who is gay, or are you talking to someone who has the ability to eternally influence many others? None of us will ever know what happens in the end until heaven answers it for us.

Life is temporary, death is eternal. I met Rich right after I officially started The Marin Foundation. He was best friends with one of the four GLBT people to attend the Foundation's very first ever spiritual acculturation class. Rich was a heavy-set man with a bald head in his mid-forties who always carried with him a thousand-watt smile. Each week Rich would drop off and pick up his best friend at class. Over the course of a few months I got to know Rich very well; he was one of the most outgoing, friendly gay men I had come in contact with to that point.

One summer day Rich randomly called me up and wanted to go out to eat in Boystown. He took me to his favorite Mexican restaurant and when we sat down he looked stressed. This was the first time Rich and I had ever hung out alone, and I thought the nerves stemmed from that. As soon as our waiter dropped off the water Rich looked at me and told me that he just found out he had AIDS.

I had no idea Rich even had HIV. He looked healthy and had plenty of meat on his bones—usually the exact opposite of what happens with someone living with HIV/AIDS. He had been HIV positive for about ten years, and his doctor told him he had become resistant to his medication. They promptly switched his meds, but those hadn't improved the situation either. His health was plummeting and he was getting nervous that he was going to die. And so with that, Rich thought the best thing to do was talk to the one religious person he knew and trusted: me.

We talked late into the evening, mostly me answering his questions. At the end of the night he teared up a little, gave me a big hug and told me that our conversation answered everything he's always wondered about but was too scared to ask. I felt good about our time and he seemed to receive everything very favorably.

That next week he once again dropped off and picked up his best friend at class. I popped my head in the car to say hi and check in. Rich gave me his classic loving smile and said, "I haven't been able to get our conversation out of my head. I had to come to a decision. I know you do such great work and help so many of my people out [GLBT people], but it's not for me."

I was sad to hear that, and to be honest it wasn't at all what I expected. I told him as much and gave him a hug. Before I left the car I said, "You know, Rich, I'll always be here if you ever want to talk about this stuff again. Anytime." I could tell that meant a lot to him.

When the class ended I would see Rich about once a month around the neighborhood for the next six months or so. But the second half of that year I didn't run in to him one time. He just never seemed to be around. I didn't really think much about it; maybe it was a timing issue or maybe he just felt like staying in more.

One year later, in June 2006, at the Gay Pride Parade I saw Rich again. He had lost what looked like half his body weight. But more apparent than anything else was the absence of his smile. All I saw was a pair of big black sunglasses hiding under a large floppy hat that covered his skin. I tried not to look too horrified, but I'm sure he could tell exactly what I was thinking. As I gave him a hug to say hello, I moved my head close to his ear and told him I was still always there for him. He took his sunglasses off and looked me in the eyes. "How could I ever forget?"

In situations like this I've come to realize that the bombardment of doctrine or the pressure of a decision is not what is needed to get an eternal point across. Presence is more than enough. A month later I got a call and I was told that Rich was in a hospice and wanted to talk. The words he said to me there are still branded in my soul.

I have known you for a while now and I never acted on what you said. But you always told me that I have until my last breath and that you'd be here for me. I am dying and on my last breath. Can you be here for me now and tell God that I am truly sorry for ignoring him? Please help me.

Rich died three days later, but not three days too late. In our last conversation Rich and I prayed. We asked for forgiveness, love and a chance to start over with such little time left. I know our Father hears those prayers, the same as he hears yours and mine. God's heart and compassion long for all of his children to seek his essence and being.

That is the essence of the Think-Big-Picture Principle. We really do have until the last breath. Rich ultimately knew when his own heart was ready to receive the Almighty. It just took him until three days before his death. But that's the point. Eternity doesn't concern *when,* it concerns *if.* The Lord will always do as he promises, and his work will continue on until its full time has been revealed.

9

Building a Bridge

Asking the Right Questions

We've laid the psychological and theological foundation to prepare the Christian community's minds to relate meaningfully to GLBT people. Our next challenge is the approach. The beginning stages of interaction are of great consequence. From moment one we must be genuine and authentic—there is no room for thinly veiled agendas.

COMMITMENT 8: AN INQUISITIVE APPROACH

Christians feel pressure to know and solve everything. Believe me I know. Pastors in particular are approached all the time for answers to all of life's unanswerable questions. And anything less than a good answer reflects poorly on their Christian leadership. That pressure to be in the know trickles down from the pulpit to the laity, so most people make an automatic association that being a good Christian also entails being definitively knowledgeable about every issue of importance to the outside world—even those issues that no one has figured out. That pressure is perceived by the broader GLBT community as arrogance. In the minds of many GLBT people, Christians believe they have all the answers, not only to life in general but to gay sexuality in particular.

It's alright—in fact it's ideal—to know that you don't have to know everything or have all of the answers to every potential aspect surrounding the topic of human sexuality. I fight almost daily the urge to come up with some theory that addresses each of the hotly contested questions of human sexuality. Our thought is that if someone would just come up with a few key answers, life would be so much easier. But God's ways are higher than human ways; the path he calls us to take often looks to us like it goes nowhere, or even goes in circles. And from God's perspective, there is no better place to be. In order to sync in to God's direct path, then, sometimes we have to let our human understanding go a little blurry.

Commitment 8—an inquisitive approach—intentionally confuses the norms of the simple answer. Many Christians believe that any talk about God will be associated by most gays and lesbians with an attack. One night at 3:45 a.m. I was peacefully writing in a twenty-four-hour Starbucks when a man tapped me on the shoulder. I didn't know who he was, but he said we went to seminary together. After a brief reintroduction he jumped right into his thought: "Everything [you] say about the GLBT community is pointless for Christians because GLBT people are brainwashed; they have no desire to listen to a Christian perspective on any issue."

Totally taken aback by what just happened, I tried to regroup my thoughts quickly. The problem for this man was that fear of a *potential* outcome had taken hold of him and skewed his understanding about how GLBT people will react. This potential fear could have come by word of mouth or through a negative experience where he tried to assert his belief system onto someone who didn't want it. Either way, however, his fear was leading him to a self-fulfilling prophecy. The way around such a crippling thought is not to speak but to listen, not to declare but to ask.

Asking and listening are more involved activities than they may seem on the surface. Certain questions don't foster conversation and can actually reinforce stereotypes and self-fulfilling prophecies—closed-ended questions that are directed toward a particular answer, rooted in rhetoric, are designed to evoke a definitive response. Gay social critic Michael Warner says that if your only tool is a hammer, every problem looks like a nail.[1] Staying away from closed-ended questions fosters an atmosphere of humility, of servanthood—neither of which are qualities usually ascribed by gays and lesbians to evangelicals.

Open-ended questions, by contrast, require not only thought but responsiveness. A great open-ended question is, "What's it like to be you?" Such a question owns the reality that heterosexual people can never fully identify with the life experience of gay people. We take the position of the eager audience. This automatically puts us in a humbled state of listening and learning. The know-it-all perception is shot out the window, and there is no better place to be in order to start building a bridge with the GLBT community.

This is not a time for rebuttals, opinions or a scriptural presence. Extending yourself to someone does more to shatter negative perceptions than any amount of oratory. Even so, I have had many gays and lesbians say to me, "OK, now that you listened to me you can tell me that I'm a sinner and I should change my behavior." They expect it, they dread it, and for the most part they cannot focus on anything else. Therefore incognito attempts at open-ended questions—whether to see if you're able to do it or not, or in an attempt to more quickly lead a person to heterosexuality—are counterproductive. No relationship can be built on fear, and true relationships do not have a hierarchy; so don't create one.

COMMITMENT 9: TRANSPARENCY & TRUTHFULNESS

Just because a person is a Christian doesn't give them an inherent right to be trusted. Christianity hasn't historically given many GLBT people the warm and comfortable feelings of being safe.

My experience has shown that it is more important to be known by gays and lesbians as being honest and vulnerable than it is to be known as a Christian. This is not blasphemy, nor is it degrading Christianity. It is rather living out the Christian faith the way it was intended to be lived. This lends itself to meeting gays and lesbians where they are, not where the Christian wants them to be.

Life is not always happy. Life doesn't always work. God doesn't always seem to be listening. Not every prayer is answered. Sometimes reading the Bible, going to church or living consistently in line with Christian tradition is difficult or even unrewarding. I call these doubts and struggles the "tangible essentials" to faith because they are real experiences in the Christian life, yet even through all of those frustrations a believer can still faithfully believe and be a child of God. Too often these tangible essentials are missing in how the faith is communicated—which is unfortunate, because they offer a neutral common ground for believers and hopeful skeptics.

A sense of mutuality fosters a spirit of reciprocity; it opens the door for either side to clearly articulate who they are and what they believe. Such dialogue is greatly advanced by an honest and transparent assessment of life, love and living for God. The Christian life must be put on trial—fair or unfair, that is what must happen. I have spent countless hours divulging my life not only to my best friends but also to random GLBT people I have just met. Nothing is too sacred. I've been told many times that I give way too much personal and intimate information, but by doing so I set the tone for my relationships. How can you expect GLBT people to share their deepest and most intimate parts of their life with nothing in return? That's why most relationships are stuck at a stagnant superficial level void of productive kingdom growth—everyone is too scared to be honest about their true colors and admit that we're in a mess together.

One of the first things I say to people is that it's fine at any time to ask me anything about anything, personally or otherwise. And in exchange I will freely give them transparently honest, personal answers and experiences. I know that is *way* easier to say than to do! I'll never forget the first few times I realized that I was way in over my head, extremely out of place and completely terrified out of my mind:

- my first two visits to a gay club—it was the Friday Night Shower Contest and Saturday Night Lube Wrestling
- the first time I was invited to speak about God at a secular GLBT HIV/AIDS and gay equality rights conference
- the first time I was interviewed on a nationally syndicated gay radio show
- the first time I was publicly slandered in the national media by someone I thought was a friend
- the first time I got an anonymous death threat as a result of lies
- the first time a grown adult broke down in front of me
- the first time someone admitted to me that they were cheating on their spouse with a person of the same sex
- the first time I was ever asked to be a sperm-donor for a lesbian couple's first kid
- the first time a transgender person told me they wanted to take back their surgery
- the first time a gay man I knew took his own life because he couldn't reconcile his faith and sexuality, and his confused and sad family asked me for answers
- the first time I saw a GLBT person come to know the Lord
- the first time I saw someone getting raped in an alley in Boystown and had to defend the defenseless by myself
- the first time someone said to me God told them they were gay
- the first time someone said to me God told them they weren't gay
- the first time I realized my soul was no different than any of theirs

Vulnerability is not for the faint of heart. It's not for people who think they're above such things. And it's not for anyone who doesn't take transparency and truthfulness to their fullest degree. In all of those situations I was pushed beyond anything I thought I could actually handle. The only thing I knew to do was to continue to lay my life out there for everyone to see as an example of my choice to be open about all that I am so we could live it all together.

COMMITMENT 10: DON'T BE SCARED TO BE YOURSELF

I have never met a more loving community in my life than the GLBT community. Obviously there are exceptions in any community, but in general I've found that GLBT people don't care if you're skinny, hairy, fat, pimpled, a millionaire or dead broke; there is room for everyone. All they want is to give the same love to others as they want to receive for themselves. When I first immersed myself I was completely taken back by the way I was treated. I was welcomed and included in everything, like I had belonged my entire life. I continued to experience this over and over, and the more it happened to me, especially at the beginning of my immersion, the more upset I became. Their actions were supposed to be me—I was getting out-Jesused by gays and lesbians! That put a bullet in my soul. To be honest, that was the furthest thing from what I thought would happen. I expected the exact opposite.

Even though my expectations were way off I still went in with an open spirit, determined to be myself. I think about those early days and I'm overwhelmed with joy and thankfulness toward all who opened their arms and hearts to me. They didn't have to take me in or do any of what they did for me, and yet they did it with joy—an example I try to reciprocate on a daily basis.

As I related in the introduction, when my three best friends told me they were gay I blurted out all of the worst negative stereotypes that quickly came to my mind. The only thing that saved our relationship from my fifteen seconds of hate was the intent they saw behind my words. They were my best friends, and they knew that no matter what words came out of my mouth that night, my heart was in the right place. They knew I wasn't trying to do anything other than understand. And because of that, they responded with more grace than I deserved at that moment.

Regardless of a Christian's firsthand experience or knowledge of the GLBT community, meaningful conversation breaks down when Christians presume they know what their gay friends think, feel and act like. Our actions toward one another are integrated into our expectations of one another. The most difficult thing for any person to do, in fact, is to live a life distinct from social, theological and cultural expectations. Those constructs dominate our society, and many times they have a stronger influence on a person's life than anything else. Some people call this peer pressure, but I believe it's beyond that. Peer pressure is external; expectations are internal. As such, they're harder to escape. And yet God calls us to be separately ourselves. Thomas Merton relates: "For me to be a saint means to be myself. . . . Therefore the problem of sanctity and salvation is in fact the problem of finding out who I am and discovering my true self."[2]

One of the most impactful programs that The Marin Foundation runs is called Out Night. We train students at Christian universities and people and pastors at churches across the country, and then we go out at night (hence the name—clever, I know) to local GLBT bars, clubs and hangouts. The point is to give Christians a firsthand experience similar to my initial immersion. The right mindset of peaceful learning from listening to and understanding gays and lesbians on their turf indelibly changes the conversation for Christians more quickly than any other means.

One September I was running an Out Night in conjunction with a seminary and their urban studies graduate students. I was floating between the different clubs the students and staff were in, and at 1 a.m. I met up with a group of students who were having a great conversation with a group of teenage cross-dressers. I turned my head and noticed a flash of light out of the corner of my eye. Walking down the street was a young African American man with a hood pulled over his head, a hat pulled low over his eyes and his hands in his pockets. When he was about five feet away, he stopped, picked his head up and stared directly into my eyes. All I saw underneath the street lights was a baby-faced kid with two bloodshot eyes and tears running down his cheeks.

I asked him if he was all right and if he wanted to talk. He quietly shook his head from side to side, then put his head back down and continued walking. I felt bad for him, but I let him be. Then he stopped, slowly turned around and started walking back in my direction. He came right up to me and whispered with a deep southern drawl, "My name is Jamal and I'd like to talk."

Jamal shared in graphic detail about how he prostitutes himself to make money. Just an hour before we met, Jamal had been in a "bathhouse," where an older man paid him for sex and then beat him. I asked him what led him to want to be a prostitute. Out of nowhere he repeated over and over, "My uncle is a minister in Mississippi, and I have problems with God. My uncle is a minister, and I have problems with God."

Jamal was seventeen years old; he ran away from home at age sixteen because he was scared of his uncle—who was the golden child of the family whom everyone looked up to and listened to. "He never had anything but really bad stuff for people like me, even if I never had done anything with a guy before. Everyone in my church would stand up and yell and scream praising his words and waving their hands and handkerchiefs in the air, and there I was only thinking about how I could run away from that. I knew they wouldn't treat me right so I didn't even try."

For the next two hours I stood there with my arm around Jamal's shoulder. When he stopped talking he must have realized he just spilled his guts to an entire stranger. He wrinkled his eyebrows, looked at me with a confused face and asked if I was gay. I shook my head no, and he smiled, "I thought so, but I'm gay. Why are you even talking to me?"

I finally told him that no matter what his problem with God was, all God wants is for us to turn to him; he promises to help us with our pain, worries and problems. Jamal started to cry again and asked me to pray that he might learn to love God and that his pain might be taken away. And so, joined by one of the graduate students who had walked by a few minutes earlier, I prayed for him right there on the street corner outside of that city's largest gay club.

When we finished he wiped his face with his sleeve and said, "You have no idea what this means to me mister. Thank you." And with that he turned and started to walk away once more. But once more he stopped, turned around and said, "I'm going to call my uncle tomorrow and go to church. Maybe God doesn't hate me."

I was able to connect Jamal with some of the students in that city, and from what I am told he has quit prostituting himself, is getting his GED, has reconnected with his family in Mississippi (including his uncle, who admitted that he had feared Jamal was gay), and is now going to church and feeling safe again. Jamal's expectations of what God felt about gay people, and what an active gay person was supposed to be like, had left him in a new city with no money and no options but to build a new, very destructive life based on those misguided expectations—which amounted to selling himself to men and living apart from family and from God. If Jamal could have only been real with his uncle, prompted by his uncle first being real with him, Jamal would not have let his erroneous expectations dictate his entire being, drifting further away from anything he once knew to be true.

Authenticity is an expression of love. As such, it's an expression of God's calling on our lives. Humble sincerity can mean more to a GLBT person than any forceful set of religious beliefs. To all people in all situations in all ways, the Christian community must honestly, authentically, sincerely and humbly represent ourselves, our beliefs and our actions as the bearers of Christ's message.

10

Crossing a Bridge

The World Reads Christians, Not the Bible

A few friends of mine were born in other parts of the world and are able to speak a variety of languages fluently. From what they tell me, English is not the easiest language to grasp—especially Chicago slang. "Bad" means "good," "sick" means "awesome," "bomb" means "great," and my personal favorite, "mug," which can mean anything I deem fit for a particular moment in time.

When it comes to bridge building with the GLBT community, one pair of words can't be made interchangeable: "no" can't mean "know."

COMMITMENT 11: DON'T *NO* THEM, *KNOW* THEM

Bridge building is not evangelism. Bridge building is a sustainable friendship, a relationship, a bond, camaraderie, closeness and strong confidence. Truly knowing a gay or lesbian person is learning to discover their social and spiritual selves through mutual respect and trust. Knowing GLBT people is the same as understanding their life from their perspective through their filtration system.

I recently read a press release sent out by a well-known Christian activist who argues that using *orientation* to describe people with same-sex attraction is a capitulation to the gay agenda. But in the minds of gays and lesbians, sexual identity is too complex, too intimate to be adequately contained in the word *lifestyle*. So just like the word *homosexual*, if you know the word is harmful and causes angst and division, then just stay away from it—say "no" to it.

I have had many GLBT people ask me why Christians, when talking about sin, compare them to murderers and drug dealers. A good friend of mine, Ramiro Medrano, has worked with murderers and drug dealers in inner-city Los Angeles and Chicago for the last twenty years and recently pointed out to me that murderers and drug dealers don't like to be associated with gay people either. Associating sins with one another doesn't help a person address their need for God. Many Christians believe that the most efficient way to communicate a deep theological point is by making an associative generalization, but general associations devalue a GLBT person's unique significance.

Christians, it's broadly supposed, are more well known for what they're against than what they're for. The main reason non-Christian gay people sense the gulf between them and God is because they, like everyone else, feel that unconscious urge of their total being— sin and all—to be reconciled to God once and for all. If our goal is to help someone know something, we have to at least temporarily forgo the "no." I am not suggesting a utopian free-for-all where everything goes. I am rather focusing on the knowledge that language, and how it's expressed, will carry a lot of weight—by holding a perception of eternity in its balance.

COMMITMENT 12: GLASS HALF-FULL

A simple rule of thumb I live my life by: a glass half-full is always better than a glass half-empty. My faith has raised me to believe that mountains can be moved. There was a time when I had nothing. I quit a comfortable job to start The Marin Foundation. I invested my entire life, financial and spiritual, into this vision I felt the Lord set before me. At one point, about a year after receiving our not-for-profit status, we had $16 total. No church was willing to take a chance on a twenty-four-year-old kid. Only my family and

GLBT people supported what I was doing. The broader Christian community thought I was nuts, but many gays and lesbians experienced life in Christ for the first time through the work of the Foundation.

There I was, qualifying for food stamps, no haircuts, no new clothes. At one time I made five boxes of rice last over a three-month period. I trusted that with God the glass is always at least half-full, even when I can only see the last drop evaporating from the bottom of the glass. As Dr. David Yonggi Cho, pastor of the world's largest church (located in Korea, with 875,000 members), says, "Realists don't change the world; dreamers do. Therefore become pregnant with a vision and birth it." You can only do that if you take Jesus at his word: "Ask and it will be given to you; seek and you will find; knock and the door will be opened to you. For everyone who asks receives; he who seeks finds; and to him who knocks, the door will be opened" (Mt 7:7-8).

Over the years I've never had any room to let failure creep into my head because this task is too big to survive in doubt. Through it all I've seen the Lord provide enough every month for the first three years of the Foundation's existence, even when I didn't know where the donations were coming from. I've seen God work in the lives of gays and lesbians. I've seen God work in the lives of Christians. Therefore I won't stop asking. I won't stop seeking. I won't stop knocking. And I won't stop believing that God pursues people who are gay and asks his people to do the same.

Commitment 12 is so important because positively reaching across a divide is abnormal, and in contemporary culture what is normal determines what is acceptable. Many people believe a glass that is half-full is, barring some kind of intervention, on its way to becoming empty. Seeing it as half-full requires an extra dose of energy. But when we choose to believe that we can talk to one another and grow toward God together, and that God can do miraculous, transformative things through us and among us, we continually depend on God to fill our cup and keep us flowing.

COMMITMENT 13: GOD'S TIMETABLE

Sexual behavior modification, "change" as it's commonly referred to, is the most pervasive fighting point between the Christian and GLBT communities. Change is a hallmark of traditional Christian faith—the idea that we can do all things through Christ who strengthens us, even refashion parts of our life that we thought were unchangeable. But when referring to sexual behavior, "change" in the classic sense of the word can't occur simply by an act of will on the part of the Christian community. Frivolous behavior modification by gays and lesbians does not stick either, and it's too easy for both sides to get anxious when results aren't immediately forthcoming.

"With the Lord a day is like a thousand years, and a thousand years are like a day" (2 Pet 3:8). It hurts my head just trying to grasp what that means for my life, let alone the life of someone that I might be tempted to map out. At the end of the day we have to let go of the timelines that make sense to us because they do nothing more than box God into our limited perspective.

You might see some change in a person's life as you interact with them over time, or you might not. But neither of those things means that you haven't walked faithfully the whole length of the journey. Instead of being swayed by any number of variables that can tear Christians off God's designated path for our relationships, a journey on God's timetable allows Christians to intently focus on their love as an orientation. Love's orientation is not defined by other people or even ourselves; it's defined by our Lord's "new command" that tells us to "love one another" (Jn 13:34-35). This is to be the sign that gives away our allegiance to the one we represent, in full submission to him and his path for other people's lives.

Love is an orientation that doesn't scrutinize; rather, it observes. It doesn't pick GLBT people's lives apart, call down judgment on them or, conversely, give them dispensation to be and do whatever they want. Love doesn't dismiss bad behavior or even outright falsehood, but love actively, concretely seeks the best for another.

Striking that fine balance is difficult. It can only come after being convinced that we have been released to love freely in conjunction with the knowledge that in another's life, God is rightfully utilizing his time in enigmatic ways. Thomas Merton suggests that the person who embraces God's vision in this way "stands receptive before the world. He no longer grabs but caresses, he no longer bites, but kisses." The body of Christ is being petitioned to stand receptive, yearned after as God longs for the moment when his children allow their grasp of love to be outlined by him—that we might once again return to Jesus' original call to his disciples, as we continue on in the GLBT community loving one another on his timetable as God has so done with us.

COMMITMENT 14: YOU ARE NOT THE SOLUTION

People in need sometimes turn to resources they know will always reliably be there for them: counselors, friends, family or pastors. The comfort that comes with being able to see a face and feel an immediate reaction and, in the case of trained and professional counselors, informed insight into their lived reality, can be among the most valuable of healing tools. But as people find themselves deeply involved in another person's spiritual journey, there can be a very real risk that the more mature Christian becomes not an aid but an easy answer to pain or a quick fix to questions and uncertainty.

The volatile history between sexuality and religion in the GLBT community has left scars on people that run deeper than anyone might reasonably be expected to address. The hierarchy that is created from this scenario puts an unhealthy expectation and responsibility on the more mature believer, often resulting in burnout for them—and often a sense of abandonment or betrayal for the other person. The higher someone is put on a pedestal the quicker a nasty collapse will follow.

The way to work around such a situation is by focusing on the individual's choice to grow their one-on-one relationship with the Lord. As the Oneness Principle reminds us, when we consciously place God first, we are necessarily committing ourselves to an alignment behind him. That's an individual responsibility—one that we can't bear for another person or assign to them.

If love is an unconditional set of measurable behaviors, it is put to the test most starkly when Christians are confronted with an outcome many of them least expect—when, for example, their gay friend tells them, "I have listened to God as you have showed me, and he told me it's OK to be gay." Our instinct is to fight, to defend a traditional interpretation of God's posture toward homosexuality. But to respond in such a way, no matter how well intentioned, is to step in between the other person and God. And whether or not GLBT people hear such a thing from God, the final factor that will usher someone into eternity is through their ability to stand on their own two feet as a believer and account for their life according to their one-on-one relationship with the Father. This understanding might seem passive to some Christians. However, such a strong will to be the salvation solution for our gay friends has the unintended consequence of turning a person's legitimate spiritual journey into a forced single moment of crisis that the person might not be ready to handle.

In the book *God in the Flesh* Don Everts comments on Jesus' last conversation with the apostle Peter:

> After breakfast Jesus has a question for Peter. Only one question.
> I probably would have asked Peter if he was going to deny me again. Or if he was feeling drowsy again. (I can be pretty sarcastic.) If I were Jesus and were about to hand Peter the authority to start and lead my church on earth, I would want to know if he was going to be more stable, more strong, more consistent. But no. Jesus has only one question for Peter. A simple one: *Do you love me?*
> Do you love me?
> He asks three times. And three times Peter says that he does. And three times Jesus calls him to "feed his sheep." Peter's new role and authority, Jesus asserts, do not rest on his strength and consistency and oaths but on his love for Jesus. . . .

Jesus wanted Peter to remember what it was really all about. And I think he did.[1]

Jesus was reminding Peter that instead of relying on his strong characteristics that very well could have done an adequate job in creating and leading God's will for what church was meant to be, Peter was to refocus his efforts back to the point of origin where the journey began—in a love for and reliance on a belief in God that he will do as he so promised. Peter's mission, as is ours today within the GLBT community, carries more weight and is filled with more love in God's eyes then we'll ever be able to grasp. Therefore the only way to faithfully carry out such a heavy calling is to place it back on the Creator who commissioned such a work. By reminding ourselves that we're not the solution to a person's salvation, we re-crown the King in his rightful place as the center of each person's relationship.

COMMITMENT 15: STREET CREDIBILITY

If the Christian community is serious about relating meaningfully to the GLBT community the most important thing the body can do is to earn "street cred." When I first started The Marin Foundation I realized that I could go to Christian churches, organizations and universities all day long, but if what I was saying had no impact with gays and lesbians, everything would be pointless. So then I stayed right in the middle of the GLBT community. I actually started to like the name people in the clubs in Boystown gave me as they got to know me: Straighty Straighterson. I became the reversal of the token gay guy that everyone loved; I was the token straight guy that everyone loved.

When it finally became broadly known in those circles that I was an evangelical Christian, people didn't reject me but rather started seeking me out with questions about God. I didn't have to do anything to facilitate such conversations. Their prejudices about evangelical Christianity didn't matter, because they had already known me for two years as Straighty Straighterson, a loving, nonthreatening straight guy who always hung out with them. Four years after that, I started The Marin Foundation, and we've been able to steadily grow because we already had years of credibility built up in the gay and lesbian community—starting in Chicago and now building around the country.

Four times in the New Testament, Jesus is shown "teaching in *their* [the Jewish] synagogues" (Mt 4:23; 9:35; Mk 1:39; Lk 4:15). Jesus didn't keep to himself or teach only disciples already committed to him. Jesus visited hostile, skeptical and even controversial people on their turf, knowing that sitting back and waiting for people to come to him was not enough.

Christian critics of organizations like The Marin Foundation— that work alongside gay and lesbian organizations—base their critique on three perceived risks.

- They believe that working with GLBT organizations will compromise the traditional Christian perspective on sexuality.

- They presume that by associating with GLBT organizations we send a message to the GLBT community that we accept their worldview.

- They fear that working with GLBT organizations lays the groundwork for Christian youth to become gay or lesbian.

I look at relationships with gays and lesbians differently than most—as a wonderful opportunity to prove my faith by reclaiming the word *love* as I tangibly live out all I believe in Christ. Fear cripples Christian bridge building. This is the same fear that was the driving force behind the attacks on Jesus' associations with people who belonged to the nontraditional sects of his day. In John 11:48 the Jews went to the Pharisees about their fear of the way Jesus lived his life, and the Pharisees thought it would ultimately bring harm to them:

> If we let him go on like this, everyone will believe in him, and then the Romans will come and take away both our place and our nation.

The Jews and the Pharisees were so crippled by the credibility Jesus had built up through his daily actions that they missed out on living and learning from the same Savior that came to die for them. But what an example for Christians today: a strange Jewish man with a unique calling saw fit to conduct his daily life by earning credibility with society's lowly outcasts one at a time. Jesus was the first true grassroots movement. Much the same, a similar opportunity within the GLBT community is waiting for us to embark on it: one unassuming Straighty Straighterson at a time who steps out to earn their street credibility one GLBT person at a time. Another grassroots kingdom movement in the making.

COMMITMENT 16:
ALWAYS ANSWER THE TOUGH QUESTIONS

The Bible will always be tied to homosexuality. The focal point of GLBT-Christian relations is irrevocably linked to a set of questions that both communities not only ask each other, but have already each assigned their own right answers.

- Do you think that gays and lesbians are born that way?
- Do you think homosexuality is a sin?
- Can a GLBT person change?
- Do you think that someone can be gay *and* Christian?
- Are GLBT people going to hell?

Since the core questions will always be the same, we must know how to respond to them in a way that elevates the conversation. Being able to answer in an elevated fashion fosters the continuance of productive dialogue and can have a twofold effect: (a) it puts an end to either community using these questions as a trap; and (b) it further facilitates a deeper social, biblical and relational exploration within the context of a sustainable relationship. These traditional "difficult conversations" will always arise, but if a sustainable relationship has been built at the core of such difficult conversations, the initial reaction of either party won't be to get up and leave.

With so much pressure and weight given to these five "litmus test" questions and their responses, the only place to turn to for guidance as an example on how to handle this kind of situation is Jesus. Throughout the Gospels Jesus was asked closed-ended questions twenty-five times by both his friends and enemies—eight times by the disciples, five by the Pharisees, four by the chief priests, four by Pilate, and one time each by John the Baptist, the Jews, Sadducees, and the woman at the well.

Closed-Ended Questions Asked of Jesus

Matthew 11:2-6	John the Baptist sends his diciples to ask Jesus if he was the one to come.
Matthew 12:10-12	The Pharisees try to trap Jesus about healing on the Sabbath.
Matthew 15:12-14	Jesus is questioned by the disciples about upsetting the Pharisees.
Matthew 19:3-6	The Pharisees question Jesus about divorce.
Matthew 19:25-26	The disciples question Jesus on who can be saved.
Matthew 21:23-27	Jesus is questioned by the chief priests and the elders on who gave him authority.
Matthew 22:17-21	The Pharisees question Jesus about paying taxes to Caesar.
Matthew 22:28-33	The Sadducees question Jesus about marriage at the resurrection.
Mark 10:10-12	The disciples ask Jesus questions about divorce.
Luke 12:41-48	Peter questions Jesus about whether he tells certain parables to just the disciples or to everyone.
Luke 22:67-69	Jesus is questioned before the chief priests about whether he is Christ.
John 4:11-14	The woman at the well asks Jesus if he is greater than Jacob.

John 6:25-27	A crowd in search of Jesus finds him on the other side of the lake and asks when he got there.
John 8:19	The Pharisees ask about the validity of Jesus' testimony.
John 8:25	The Pharisees ask Jesus who he is.
John 8:52-56	The Jews question Jesus about who he thinks he is.
John 11:8-9	The disciples ask Jesus if he's really going to go to Lazarus back in Judea.
John 13:6-7	Simon Peter asks Jesus if he's going to wash Peter's feet.
John 18:33-34	Pilate questions Jesus about his kingship.
John 18:35-36	Pilate asks Jesus what he's done.
John 19:9-11	Pilate questions Jesus again about Pilate's power.

Yes-No Responses from Jesus

Matthew 21:16	Jesus is questioned by the chief priests after he heals the blind and the lame in the temple area and children shout "Hosanna to the Son of David." He answers "yes" and then quotes Psalm 8:2.
Matthew 26:63-64	When Jesus is on trial before the Sanhedrin they ask if he is Christ. He answers "yes."
Matthew 27:11	Jesus answers "yes" to Pilate when Pilate asks if he is the king of the Jews.
John 9:1-5	After healing the blind man Jesus answers the disciples' question to counter a legalistic tradition.

Out of those twenty-five times, fifteen of them were Jesus' enemies trying to shrewdly trap him in his own words. Yet only once during his three-year public ministry, prior to his arrest and trial, did Jesus answer a closed-ended question with a closed-ended answer (Mt 21:16). Instead of responding to his antagonizers through the traditional means, Jesus counterculturally reframed each question in such a way that brought intentionality to overarching kingdom principles.

Such was the case when the Pharisees tried to test Jesus on his doctrine of divorce (Mt 19:3-9; Mk 10:2-9). They were seeking a simple answer for their legalistically based question of the lawfulness of a man being allowed to divorce his wife for any and every reason—fully knowing that Moses allowed a man to send a woman away with a certificate of divorce. Jesus knew their intentions, and instead of giving the Pharisees the politically charged legalistic answer they expected, he shifted the focal point of his response onto the larger kingdom issue of adultery, rooted in the Pharisees' realm of knowledge—the Ten Commandments.

None of Jesus' refocused responses to his enemies were void of passion. Just because he shifted the context of the closed-ended questions from legal to eternal, he wasn't going to roll over in his convictions. He was merely refusing to treat a complex question simplistically—which is the biblical basis for elevating the conversation in similar situations that Christians find themselves in today with the GLBT community. What about the other two times that Jesus did respond to his enemies with a traditional closed-ended answer? In both of those cases (Mt 26:63-64; 27:11) Jesus was already on trial and his time of public ministry had come to an end. There was no more need at that point to counterculturally reach out, stay alive or teach any more eternal principles. Jesus understood that his time on earth was complete, and there was just one task still ahead of him—to fulfill the prophecies of the Old Testament on the cross.

But Jesus didn't resist closed-ended questions only from his critics. The Gospels record ten times when his followers asked him closed-ended questions, and only one of those times did Jesus offer a closed-ended response (Jn 9:1-5). The other nine times Jesus once again reframed each closed-ended question to orient it toward a more thorough understanding. In fact, the very first recorded time that Jesus was ever asked a closed-ended question was by John the Baptist—the one to prepare the way for the Savior—wondering if Jesus was the one to come (Mt 11:2-3). Setting the tone for what would be the duration of his three-year public ministry, Jesus did not respond with the harmlessly desired "yes" or "no" longed for by John the Baptist.

> Go back and report to John what you hear and see: The blind receive sight, the lame walk, those who have leprosy are cured, the deaf hear, the dead are raised, and the good news is preached to the poor. Blessed is the man who does not fall away on account of me. (Mt 11:4-6)

Jesus did answer the question—as he did the others—but in each situation he did so in an elevated fashion that brought light to the larger kingdom issues that led God to ultimately send his Son to die for humanity's sin. The same principles Jesus used with his enemies he also used with those closest to him. This unmistakably demonstrates Jesus' commitment to sticking with the process that he thought best. And if it's good enough for Jesus it's good enough for me. So with Jesus as our guide, let's consider how we can crack open the closed-ended questions that pervasively surround homosexuality and the Christian belief.

Do you think that gays and lesbians are born that way? If I were to answer yes or no, I would earn the endorsement of one community at the expense of the trust of the other community. And frankly, as plain and simple as I can possibly put it: I don't care if gays and lesbians are or aren't born that way. Is that too harsh? My opinion one way or the other won't bring an end to nor advance the frantic genetic and behavioral research taking place to try to find out which one is true. And whether they're born gay or straight, they are created to be a child of God. Just as Jesus refocused the closed-ended questions asked of him back onto kingdom principles, here is a reframed question in the same fashion: "How do you think your genetic makeup relates to God's desire to be called your Father?"

Do you think homosexuality is a sin? This is the most loaded of all of the loaded questions. Romans 3:23, however, says that "all have sinned and fall short of the glory of God." Other than the Son, no one—gay or straight, Christian or non-Christian—can match the standard laid out for us by the Father. In fact, James 2:10 says that "whoever keeps the whole law and yet stumbles at just one point is guilty of breaking all of it." In other words, from God's perspective if you've committed one sin it's like you've committed them all. Think about what that really means for a second. If everyone is a sinner, and if James 2:10 is actually true (which I believe it is), then in God's eyes we're all the same—Christian or non-Christian, gay or straight. So where has the dissension come from, since we're all the same? And Matthew 7:1-2 says, "Do not judge, or you too will be judged. For in the same way you judge others, you will be judged, and with the measure you use, it will be measured to you." The last thing I would ever want to have happen is for God to judge me the same way I judge other people—especially how I judged the GLBT community the first nineteen years of my Bible-banging homophobic life!

The good news is that the final determining factor of a person's eternal security is not the achievement of sinlessness but the establishment of a one-on-one relationship with God. It's a matter of faith and integrity. I honestly believe that everyone is trying to figure out how to live with understanding and meaning and purpose. Here are a few ways to reframe the question: "How do you relate to a God whose standards are so unachievable? How do you deal with the moral vulnerability we all have to live with? What does it mean to you that such a perfect God still wants to be in relationship with imperfect beings such as us?"

Can a GLBT person change their sexual orientation? I believe change happens when Jesus gets hold of someone's life. Who knows, however, what kind of change it might turn out to be? It might not be the same change that the Christian community automatically thinks of when they hear that word referencing sexuality, but change does happen. The metric of change in relation to a GLBT person's faith journey has traditionally been black and white: gay or not gay; success or failure. But I see a continuum of change that can cover a number of variables:

- secular to spiritual
- non-Christian to Christian
- sexually active to celibate
- gay to straight
- somewhere in between any of the others

Also, sticking to facts diffuses the weight of opinion-based answers. Therefore I continue answering the question with: "I also know some people who say that they once had same-sex sexual attraction but are now attracted exclusively to people of the opposite sex, and in fact are married and have kids and are living a happy life. Just the same I know people who have tried and tried and tried, and have not been able to 'change their sexual orientation,' and therefore have stopped trying and are actively involved in the GLBT community. All these people from both life experiences are telling the truth as they perceive it, and each falls somewhere different on the spectrum of change."

Meanwhile, in a relationship with God we ought to expect changes in our lives well beyond our sexuality. People's religious identity, like their sexual identity, will also fall somewhere on a continuum of change reflective of God's work in their life, as all of life's intricacies either positively or negatively influence each person's oneness with God. Regardless of how a gay or lesbian person's life changes—religiously, sexually or otherwise—will not be finalized until their last breath, just like everyone else. Here are a few more productively reframed questions: "What do you think is changing in your life as a result of where you're at in relation to God? Where do you think God wants to move you on your own personal continuum of change?"

Do you think that someone can be gay and Christian? My immediate thought is, what is stopping such a person from believing? The focus rightly belongs not on a yes-or-no question but on the hang-ups, doubts, negative experiences or theological difficulties that are inhibiting a particular gay or lesbian person from believing in Christ.

Many gays and lesbians consider themselves to be gay Christians, just as many people who have same-sex attraction believe that GLBT people actively indulging their same-sex attraction cannot truly be Christians. It's impossible to definitively assess the deep crevices of a person's heart. Ultimately anyone involved in the Christian community—gay or straight, Christian or non-Christian—should be taken at their word about where they spiritually find themselves because only God really knows someone's faith and the intent behind all their actions. It's not our job to convict. It's not our job to judge. It's our job to love. In a reframed manner then: "What religious and cultural barriers have you experienced as a GLBT person regarding belief in Christ? What does the term 'gay Christian' mean to you and how has that impacted your life?"

Are GLBT people going to hell? I am once again brought to Jesus' words related in Matthew 7:21-23. The fear of eternity stares us all in the face, and my opinions are not going to get anyone into heaven, and by extension, they're not going to land anyone in hell. Only God can accomplish either of those things. And since he is the ultimate Judge, a whole lifetime of seeking his face and listening to his voice would be a life well spent. The privilege of entering God's kingdom only comes through his acknowledgment of an authentic relationship with him.[2] It's up to God, not us. Therefore judgments of heaven and hell reframed can be asked as: "What scares you about hell? How would you make the case for God to let you into heaven?"

Generally speaking, I don't know any believer—gay or straight—who doesn't want to be like Jesus. And here is our chance to be just a little more like him: stop asking and answering closed-ended questions in an attempt to determine if someone is on "our team" or "their team." Jesus modeled a life about kingdom ways and thinking, not pinning down—or getting pinned down by—circularly legalistic debates of politically charged matters. As such we have the ability to follow his model and elevate our questions and answers past the same means that have tragically only haunted the GLBT-Christian relationship.

Conclusion

Every stereotype can be broken with a face, and every face has a story. Even leaders in both the GLBT and the Christian community tell me they know that something needs to change—but nothing is changing because we've all been conditioned to dig in and fight. So where are we to go from here?

The uniqueness of the Christian faith is its call to be distinct, walking in a way that sidesteps social and cultural norms. But the Christian faith calls for a specific distinction: love. Theologian Francis Schaeffer believed that love is the indelible mark that God gave to Christians to wear before the world: "Only with this mark may the world know that Christians are indeed Christians and that Jesus was sent by the Father."[1] So we're called by Christ to be different by being loving—by choosing humility over hostility, by braving the unknown rather than huddling in safe enclaves, by daring to face people who we've offended and who have offended us, and inviting them into a reconciled relationship with God and one another.

> All this is from God, who reconciled us to himself through Christ and gave us the ministry of reconciliation: that God was reconciling the world to himself in Christ, not counting men's sins against them. And he has committed to us the message of reconciliation. We are therefore Christ's ambassadors, as

though God were making his appeal through us. We implore
you on Christ's behalf: Be reconciled to God. (2 Cor 5:18-20)

We're not called to posit theories that support our assumptions.
We're not called to speculate about genetics or developmental experiences or spiritual oppression in faceless groups of other people.
We're called to build bridges informed by the Scriptures and em-
powered by the Spirit. We're called to let a just God be the judge of
his creation. We're called to let the Holy Spirit whisper truth into
each person's heart. And we're called to show love unconditionally,
tangibly, measurably.

Five years into my immersion experience, shortly after I started
The Marin Foundation, I received a phone call from a gay organization. They asked me if I wanted to speak about God at their upcom-
ing conference. I quickly said yes, but as soon as I hung up the
phone I was scared out of my mind. This would be my first time
speaking in front of hundreds of GLBT people at one time—the vast
majority of whom had absolutely no idea who I was or what I was all
about. I wasn't sure how I could quickly and succinctly explain my
message. And I was straight. And I was evangelical. And I was only
twenty-five years old.

About four hundred people attended the conference. Among the
other speakers were a well-known politician who supported gay
rights and a lesbian woman who had recently been nominated for a
Nobel Peace Prize. Sweating profusely, I took the stage and stood at
the podium looking out over a ballroom full of gay, lesbian, bisexual
and transgender people with half-polite smiles, half-puzzled faces,
wondering what in the world I was doing there.

For the next hour and fifteen minutes I talked about my goal of
building a bridge between the GLBT and conservative religious communities while still acknowledging the social and theological differences between the two. The next thing I knew my audience was
on their feet. But they were clapping, not walking out! I couldn't
believe it.

At the opposite end of the ballroom was a table set up so I could answer questions. Hesitantly I sat down with a couple bottles of water in front of me and thought, *Now they're going to let me have it.* I was shocked by the large number of people in line, including an odd-looking pair standing at the very back. On the left was a 6'6" African American man who couldn't have been more than a hundred pounds soaking wet, talking to a little 5'3" elderly Asian woman. After about an hour of questioning, everyone else had left, and these two worked their way up to the table. When I said hi the African American man spread his large hands over the table, leaned in and said, "You know, we're atheists and gay, and we could have cared less about what you had to say."

You waited all of this time just to say that? Not knowing what else to do, I smiled and thanked them for listening. I started to pack up my belongings, but they kept standing in front of the table staring at me. Maybe they just didn't understand nonverbal body language cues? I looked up again, took a nervous deep breath and smiled at them one more time. This time the elderly Asian lady added, "We live outside the city. The only reason we stayed to hear you speak was because our train didn't leave until after you were going to be completed. So we stayed to waste some time."

Can this get any worse? I was just hoping they would walk away and leave me alone. But they kept standing there in silence looking intently at me. I finished packing my things, shrugged my shoulders and meekly asked if they had anything else to say.

Then a tear began to slowly creep down the right side of the man's cheek. He quickly tucked his hand into his sleeve and wiped the tear from his chin. Why was he crying? The woman stood in place for what seemed to be a lifetime, rotating her head from him to me, from him to me, from him to me.

I got up and walked around the table and stood right next to the African American man. I wasn't sure what I was supposed to do or say, so I stood there in silence. After wiping his eyes for the second time he looked me dead in the face and said, "I came here as an atheist, and I want to leave knowing what it is like to make a cognizant decision for God. Can you help me understand what that means?"

Now it was my turn to cry. The woman just seemed to fade away in the background, leaving him to be there with me. I gave him a hug and we sat down, and I started answering his questions. By the end of the night we exchanged information, and that next week I helped plug him into a great church where he lived. We keep in touch a few times a year; he's still attending that church and continuing to explore a journey with the God of the Bible.

That night in my hotel room I couldn't fall asleep. I was so rattled by what happened with that African American man. I mean, it's not like I had never seen anyone cry or come to Christ before. What made this time so different? And then it hit like a ton of bricks: This was the very first time I had witnessed someone whom I didn't know, who didn't know me, whom I hadn't been in a sustainable relationship with, make an eternal choice for God and all that comes with him.

About a month later I was asked to appear on a nationally syndicated Christian radio show to talk about my experience at that GLBT conference. The director of the radio show had heard a download of my presentation from the conference. I couldn't figure out why they would want to talk about it, and when I asked he said, "In all my life I have never heard of anything like this before. When was the last time a conservative evangelical Christian was given the opportunity to share their heart and passion for God with hundreds of radically political GLBT people and not have anything violent or bad occur? That just doesn't happen. It was literally a miracle."

His words sunk deep in my soul, and at that moment I realized that God used my willingness to fly across the country and step into an extremely uncomfortable environment—where by all understanding I did not belong—to bring the right message at the right time, so that one gay atheist could believe. All God needs are willing hearts to extend his unconditional love for all of his children—gay and straight. This is our blessing. This is our bold calling. This is our orientation.

Appendix

Testimonies from the Gay Community

Throughout this book I have tried to usher you into what has become my daily existence within the gay, lesbian, bisexual, transgender and religious communities. Over the years I have had the humble privilege of rooting myself in the place of tension that many gays and lesbians experience with their journeys of faith. Their lives are complex, and the people you'll meet in the stories that follow are each living out their journey from a different place than the others—whether celibate, ex-gay or gay Christian. As the body of Christ continues to learn how to peacefully and productively build bridges with the GLBT community, we must live, as a friend of mine from the U.K. says, "in the now and the not yet." Let your heart be opened by my friends' words as they tell you about their lives. Pray that each of us will one day be able to encounter such a life, fostering meaningful and sustainable relationships that make a significant impact for the kingdom of our heavenly Father.

■ ■ ■

Gandhi once said, "I like your Christ. I do not like your Christians. Your Christians are so unlike your Christ." As I think about the thirty years I have spent reconciling my Christianity with my sexuality, I am comforted knowing that I am not the only one with a less than stellar assessment of other Christians. Accepting the Lord as a teenager, I clearly did not realize that the next thirty years would be spent in a battle to gain a sense of purpose and value as a woman in the church. The Proverbs 31 virtuous individual so cherished by the body of Christ was out of my grasp; I would have neither a husband or children to bless me.

The first time I became aware of my attraction to girls, I was twelve years old. I did not share my feelings with anyone until I became attracted to my best friend at sixteen years of age. The feelings were mutual and we embarked on a physical and emotional relationship. Three months later we were introduced to Christ. From that moment on, we knew that something was now very wrong with our relationship, but we had neither the context nor counselors to help us navigate through our feelings and friendship.

I am not saying that I actually believed we were wrong. I didn't know. What I am saying is that the very fragile beginning of my present rich relationship with the Lord was marked by a deep sense of shame. I wish I had known a believer in Christ who would affirm that God and his people loved us and were devoted to us in our journey, regardless of the outcome.

Over the years I developed two strategies to make sense of the angst I felt about faith and sexuality. Initially, I became very religious and judgmental. Hoping God would remove my attraction for women if I would recruit those like me into heterosexuality, I found myself harsh, bitter and unloving. My second strategy developed out of a sense of hopelessness that I would forever be celibate; I became reckless and irresponsible in my sexual behavior. That short-lived period ended up in heartache, shame and regret that I gave away something I had cherished up until that time.

With two failed strategies and a persistent and nagging attraction for women, I turned to prayer, counseling and, finally, a "deliverance." But despite all of these interventions, I still felt the same. My epiphany came when a lesbian I worked with shared that her girlfriend had come out to her Catholic parents the previous weekend. I asked how it went. She replied, "It went well because, you know, we all are born this way." That night I went to God in prayer and gave him an ultimatum, as I had for many years: "Lord, I am so tired of not having a response to someone who says that gays are born that way. I am not going to go another night without a response for them or for myself." I clearly heard in my spirit, "I created you perfectly, just as you are. How you walk out your journey regarding the totality of who you are will not take away from what I have already established and cherished in creating you."

My survival mentality had only led to defensiveness and self-hatred, remnants of which still remain. What emerged that night was a deep sense of certainty that God had my back and that I was the apple of his eye, even if those in the church chose to interpret the Bible a certain way or believed they could establish a hierarchy regarding the value of people groups and Scriptures.

My prayer is that those who profess Christ as their Savior listen closely to the words of Gandhi and embrace the possibility that, by truly being more like Jesus, they could capture the minds of those in the world while healing the hearts of those in the church.

■   ■   ■

Seventeen years ago, my life came to a crossroad. In my mind, I could either commit suicide or give God one more chance to change my life and bring it meaning. Prior to coming to this crossroad, I had struggled with my sexual identity as well as depression and anxiety.

My earliest recollection of being attracted to men was when I was six years old. I remember fantasizing about growing up to be a woman and marrying a man. Specific males came to my mind as I considered the kind of man I would marry. They were all muscular, handsome and confident.

Later in life, I learned that these same-sex attractions were manifestations from unresolved emotional and spiritual issues in my life. I decided, at this crossroad, to commit my life to Christ and follow him. I had grown up in the church, but only at the age of twenty did I really understand that Christ died for my sins and that only through his sacrifice could I receive eternal life.

In addition, I began to understand the sanctification process, whereby sins could dissipate and weaknesses could be transformed into strengths. However, I had no idea how my sexuality was going to change. I was not connected with ministries helping individuals transition out of homosexuality, and going to counseling was a scary prospect. In fact, I didn't really think there was a possibility of changing my sexual desires. So I focused my energies on growing in my relationship with Christ. I made a commitment to celibacy, choosing to live with these same-sex desires the rest of my life.

God brought men into my life that loved me and modeled for me what it meant to be both godly and intimate, without any hint of homosexuality. Through my close relationships with these men over a period of ten years, God brought up the unresolved issues in me that needed to be addressed. Although there was no ministry around at that time to aid me in my journey, God worked through these relationships, and the body of Christ became the instrument for healing in my life.

The result was a complete change in my sexual desires from homosexuality to heterosexuality. Today I am married and have two sons. I believe that what I experienced in the church should be the norm. Sadly, it is not. From my observations and work with men and women coming out of homosexuality for the past sixteen years, most have *not* had the kind of experience I had, where individuals were a tremendous support helping bring about healing and trans-formation. For many, experiences of rejection, neglect and ignorance in counsel have been pervasive.

One of my desires serving as a pastor is to be a voice for the gay community, speaking to the ways Christians have sinned against gays and lesbians, and to be a living example of how to love anyone while remaining faithful to the message of the gospel. Christ came to bring healing and transformation in many ways, but I believe many Christians have not experienced this for themselves, nor do they hope for this healing for others in the world. We need to be re-ignited with the passion of Christ and see how he can be real in a world where there is much confusion about sexuality.

■ ■ ■

As a gay evangelical Christian I am a man without a country. I am too much of a Christian to fit into the secular gay community. There's nothing that would make me want to be a part of a bar scene. I have no intention of becoming flamboyant, campy, promiscuous or a substance abuser. I have no intention or desire to change anything about who I am. And such change isn't inevitable. It doesn't go hand-in-hand with allowing myself to accept this orientation. My orientation is already a part of who I am and who I am becoming.

Accepting my orientation makes me unwelcome in my own Christian circles. Within the United Methodist Church, of which I am a member, I cannot serve in ministry as an openly gay person. In some bodies I could be denied a leadership position and even membership. In some churches that consider themselves more progressive and compassionate, I would be allowed to sit in a pew as long as I kept my mouth shut and stayed away from the kids.

The fact that I have been a church member in good standing for thirty years, and the fact that I have been participating in some sort of ministry for over twenty-five years, and the fact that I am seminary trained, and the fact that I have gifts, talents and abilities which I have been using to minister to others—and last but not least, the fact that my relationship with the Lord is the most important thing in my life—all of this means nothing because of my orientation. And that sucks.

So, my prayer is that the Lord will lead me to a place where I can fit. I need fellowship with other Christians but also with others who share my orientation. And I need to do the ministry I'm called to do. There are so many people out there who share my orientation and feel isolated and alone. There are people hiding in the church and those who feel rejected by the church. I envision a flock of sheep scattered and left to fend for themselves.

Perhaps my ministry is to shepherd them—to find a way to draw them back in. I pray that I find the answers to these questions soon and that I have the courage to follow the Lord's lead.

■ ■ ■

Can one be both "Christian" and "gay" at the same time? Well, I suppose that depends on how you define the terms. If "Christian" means I trust Jesus alone to bring me into right relationship with God and if "gay" means I experience sexual attraction and romantic feelings toward people of the same sex, then I qualify as a gay Christian. At one point I *chose* to be a Christian, and over a period of time, I *discovered* I'm gay.

My Christianity informs my homosexuality more than my sexuality informs my Christianity; therefore I tend to consult the Bible regarding matters related to sexuality—not my sexual feelings regarding matters related to my Christianity. The Bible doesn't say much about sexual feelings or attractions (except when it exposes the negatives of lust). Rather, Christian Scripture speaks more of sexual *function.*

The emphasis seems to be on the nature of sexual expression as a key distinguishing element to a very unique, one-of-a-kind human relationship: marriage. Throughout Scripture people operate in a variety of relationships: they have friends, children, parents, siblings, slaves, masters, business associates, governors, subjects and enemies. Legitimate sexual expression doesn't characterize any of these relationships. Biblically, sex happens within the context of a *marital* relationship. Out of such expression, children are sometimes born and the earth is populated, but childbirth doesn't seem to be the emphasis of biblical sexual expression. Instead, as the burner makes the stove a unique appliance in the kitchen, or as a crown differentiates the queen from everyone else in the kingdom, sex is a clear marker of that one unique relationship, and the extent to which we practice it outside of marriage, we erode the significance of that unique relationship. In addition, the Bible suggests that this relationship be a covenant, lifelong, monogamous relationship, characterized by certain boundaries which no outsider should penetrate and by support from one's community.

In twenty-first-century American culture, when a newly married couple leaves the reception, everyone at the wedding expects and supports the sexual relationship into which they're about to enter. Through the years when that relationship brings a reason to celebrate (a pregnancy is announced, for example), the whole community rejoices, and if there are problems in the relationship (the couple doesn't get along), it seems to be God's intention that the community help heal and restore the relationship. Sexual relationships other than those in marriage are usually guarded with secrecy—they're not a community matter.

As a Christian then, I realize life will probably be more orderly and less chaotic for me if I decide to practice sexual expression only within the safe confines of my community-supported heterosexual marriage. There's only one problem: my feelings don't jive with that. I want to have sex with another man, not a woman.

But for me, that's all it is. One problem. One among many. I also want to have a billion dollars. I want to be healthy every single day. I always want to feel as if I've had enough sleep, and I would like to subsist on a diet of ice cream and chocolate sauce. I'd like my friends to always like me and I'd like a good relationship with my sister. And if I'm honest, I don't want to have sex with just one man—I enjoy looking at all kinds of men, and in that place within which I *desire* things, I'd like to be with many of those men.

We can't always have what we want. Right? This doesn't just apply to the Christian. This applies to everyone. I mean, go ahead and eat a diet of only ice cream and chocolate sauce for the next year, and see what happens to your health. Toss aside biblical wisdom about sexual expression and see where that gets you emotionally.

Biblical Christianity is quite fond of desire. Biblical Christianity also wrote the rule book on how desire can best be parlayed into fulfillment. One privilege afforded the Christian is the opportunity to discover healthy avenues for desire. This privilege isn't available to those who reject God. Practically, this means that I get to surrender my gay desire to Jesus and let him do with it whatever he wants.

I'm not obligated to build an entire life on the basis of this one problem. I have the opportunity to minimize the importance of so-called sexual freedom in a sexually charged society; I don't have to be a slave to sexual thoughts, appetites and practices; instead I can live an orderly, breezy, clutter-free existence, as described in Romans 8:6 *(The Message):* "Obsession with self in these matters is a dead end; attention to God leads us out into the open, into a spacious, free life."

This is the life Jesus paid so high a price for me to have. Granted, if I seek this type of life, I don't get the thrill or euphoria of multiple orgasms with multiple partners. But most people—Christian or not—don't get this either. It is likely that most people long for it a lot more than they actually get it, and if anyone slips through the cracks and actually *does* get it—outside of marriage—most likely his inner world is characterized by chaos and turmoil. This just seems to be how God designed the human.

So was it fair of God to set up his standards and then let me be gay? Again, the Bible informs my thinking on this—and the Bible teaches that God is fair. There must be some other explanation. Why do I have to be gay in a world where we're all better off keeping our sexual expression within a specific institution? Why are there diabetics and poor people and abused children? Why do earthquakes destroy homes and lives? Why is there drought? The Bible clearly teaches that ours is a *fallen* world—so it often amuses me, and more often perplexes and then discourages me, that Christians expect the world to be fair and for everything to go well all the time. It doesn't.

I think everyone must have some tough cross to bear. We all face struggles and temptations; most of us sometimes fall along the lines of our struggles, and we end up sorry for it and wishing we could have done things differently. My struggle doesn't bother me constantly—it seems to limit itself to the hours I'm awake!

Acknowledgments

The Bible is quite a book, well, more like sixty-six books that the Lord wove together to teach his children how to love, live, revere, pray and ultimately connect with him. I am always amazed by the form in which our Father decided to cement his word: a book that can be memorized and read and reread a million times over. Good concept—one that can be succinctly utilized for optimal human learning as the stories, principles and doctrine stay as consistent as the ink on the page. But in the same breath the Lord also knew that his word in book form was going to be a free-for-all for those who choose not to believe in him, or have been hurt by those who claim his name. Yet knowing exactly what was going to happen God still thought a book, or sixty-six of them, was the best way to go.

For those reasons I take writing a book very seriously. I know the words within these covers will be read and reread, dissected and picked apart by many people on both sides. The Lord has laid this opportunity before me and I feel it is my command to be faithful to this journey I have been given. Agree or disagree. At the end of the day if I have nothing else I know that I truly have peace in my spirit, knowing that I have been true to all of those people who have allowed me to live life with them along the way. And to that I cannot thank them enough.

This book is not just a product of what I have done, but of many others who have also done so much since the very first day The

Marin Foundation was brought into existence:

Thank you, Lord, for picking me up by the seat of my pants and flinging me through many thick brick walls along the way. Even though I lay dazed on the other side of the crumbled wall with little yellow birdies flying around my head, you have made a door where by all human standards, a door could never have existed. Praise your holy name.

I am truly humbled by and thankful to John Fuder, Ginny Olson, Becky Kuhn, Eric Leocadio, Phil Jackson, Christian Community Development Association, Ted Curtis, Erika Sterken, John Lewis, Larry Acosta, Urban Youth Workers Institute, the Coalition, Randy Dattoli, Jim Coakley, David Woodall, Bill Shereos, Richard Engle, Brad Grammer, Kristen Sifers, Tim Otto, Joe Piercy, Cathy Nerenberg, Adam McLane, Carla Lafayette, Celina Camarillo, Earl Hartville, Diane Hartig, Nancy Jacque, Rita Ballanger, Dawn Bodi, Nate Lam, Trammel Orr, Elaina Vazquez, Brother Clarence Walker III, Jantzen Loza, Noah Adair, Brian McLaren, all of the encouragers from my Facebook community, Steve H. at the Starbucks on North Avenue and Wells Street where I wrote this book, and of course my entire family for always being there in love and support.

Thank you to my InterVarsity Press family: Bob Fryling, Jeff Crosby, Andrew Bronson, Adrianna Wright, Heather Mascarello, Ruth Curphey, Rebecca Larson, Cindy Kiple and all of the hard working people behind the scenes who sell the books, pack the books and ship the books. Special thanks to my editor, Dave Zimmerman, who, since day one, has been as excited about this project as me—and that's a really hard thing to do.

Peter, Beth, Erwin, Jean, Michael and Carol—I am who I am because of how you raised me. From as far back as I can remember you instilled in me the belief that people were created to do great things for Christ, no matter how crazy it might seem to anyone else. Without you, none of what I do in life would ever have been a reality. I love you all so much.

There is an old cliché that says save the best for last. I'm guessing the person who coined that term was probably the perpetual "last" in everything they did. But in this case I needed to save the best for last so I could properly thank my wife, Brenda. How much can one person sacrifice and yet love in such a way that draws me closer to her, and God, each day of our lives together? You uniquely entered into this journey and have encouraged me, held me up and charged ahead full steam since the first day we met. I love you so much, and would not be able to move forward without you.

Notes

Chapter 1: We Don't Need Your God!
[1]Recent publications include Gabe Lyons and Dave Kinnaman, *unChristian* (Grand Rapids: Baker, 2007); and Dan Kimball, *They Like Jesus but Not the Church* (Grand Rapids: Zondervan, 2006).

Chapter 2: We Are Not Your Project
[1]Of course, the option of "being heterosexual" leads to its own set of constraints—celibacy, marital fidelity or a life of sexual sin. But one gets the impression from straight Christian rhetoric directed at the GLBT community that rampant heterosexual sexual irresponsibility is an acceptable substitute for even the most restrained gay sexuality.

Chapter 3: Stigma, Shame and Politics
[1]Andy Crouch, *Culture Making* (Downers Grove, Ill.: IVP Books, 2008).

Chapter 4: Gay Versus Christian and Gay Christians
[1]Jeff Miner and John Tyler Connoley, *The Children Are Free: Reexamining the Biblical Evidence on Same-Sex Relationships* (Indianapolis: Jesus Metropolitan Community Church, 2002), p. 42.
[2]Joe Dallas, *The Gay Gospel? How Pro-Gay Advocates Misread the Bible* (Eugene, Ore.: Harvest House, 2007), pp. 41, 62.

Chapter 5: Who Are We Looking to for Validation?
[1]Craig Keener, *The IVP Bible Background Commentary: New Testament* (Downers Grove, Ill.: InterVarsity Press, 1993), pp. 463-64.
[2]Michael Warner, *The Trouble with Normal* (Boston: Harvard University Press, 1999), p. 185.
[3]Shane Claiborne and Chris Haw, *Jesus for President* (Grand Rapids: Zondervan, 2008), p. 167.

[4]Ibid., p. 117.

[5]Warner, *Trouble with Normal*, p. 23.

Chapter 6: Reclaiming the Word *Love*

[1]Gabe Lyons and Dave Kinnaman, *unChristian* (Grand Rapids: Baker, 2007).

[2]John V. Richardson, "Open Versus Closed Ended Questions," accessed November 24, 2008, at <http://polaris.gseis.ucla.edu/jrichardson/dis220/openclosed.htm>.

[3]Geoffrey W. Bromiley, *International Standard Bible Encyclopedia* (Grand Rapids: Eerdmans, 1994), 3:175.

[4]R. T. France, "Matthew," in *New Bible Commentary*, ed. G. J. Wenham, J. A. Motyer, D. A. Carson and R. T. France, 21st century ed. (Downers Grove, Ill.: InterVarsity Press, 1994), p. 914.

Chapter 7: The Big 5

[1]J. Scott Duvall and J. Daniel Hays, *Grasping God's Word* (Grand Rapids: Zondervan, 2005), pp. 394-97.

[2]Ibid., p. 362.

[3]John Walton, Victor Matthews and Mark Chavalas, *The IVP Bible Background Commentary: Old Testament* (Downers Grove, Ill.: InterVarsity Press, 2000), p. 51.

[4]Craig Keener, *The IVP Bible Background Commentary: New Testament* (Downers Grove, Ill.: InterVarsity Press, 1993), p. 238.

[5]I. Howard Marshall, *New Testament Theology* (Downers Grove, Ill.: InterVarsity Press, 2004), p. 1008.

[6]John Stott, quoted in Gabe Lyons and Dave Kinnaman, *unChristian* (Grand Rapids: Baker, 2007), pp. 150-51.

[7]Robin Scroggs, *The New Testament and Homosexuality* (Minneapolis: Augsburg/Fortress, 1983), pp. 19-42.

[8]John Boswell, *Christianity, Social Tolerance, and Homosexuality* (Chicago: University of Chicago Press, 2005), pp. 70, 77.

[9]Geoffrey W. Bromiley, *International Standard Bible Encyclopedia* (Grand Rapids: Eerdmans, 1994), 3:708-9.

[10]Ibid., p. 857.

Chapter 8: Laying the Foundation

[1]Charles Swindoll and Roy Zuck, eds., *Understanding Christian Theology* (Nashville: Thomas Nelson, 2003), pp. 1025-28.

[2]David Wheaton, "1 Peter," in *New Bible Commentary*, ed. G. J. Wenham, J. A. Motyer, D. A. Carson and R. T. France, 21st century ed. (Downers Grove, Ill.: InterVarsity Press, 1994), p. 1381.

Chapter 9: Building a Bridge
[1]Michael Warner, *The Trouble with Normal* (Boston: Harvard University Press, 1999), p. 167.
[2]Thomas Merton, *New Seeds of Contemplation,* quoted in James Martin, *Becoming Who You Are* (Mahwah, N.J.: Hidden Spring, 2006), p. ix.

Chapter 10: Crossing a Bridge
[1]Don Everts, *God in the Flesh* (Downers Grove, Ill.: InterVarsity Press, 2005), p. 158.
[2]R. T. France, *The Gospel of Matthew,* New International Commentary on the New Testament (Grand Rapids: Eerdmans, 2007), p. 914.

Conclusion
[1]Francis Schaeffer, *The Mark of the Christian,* IVP Classics (Downers Grove, Ill.: IVP Books, 2006), p. 59.

LIKEWISE. *Go and do.*

A man comes across an ancient enemy, beaten and left for dead. He lifts the wounded man onto the back of a donkey and takes him to an inn to tend to the man's recovery. Jesus tells this story and instructs those who are listening to "go and do likewise."

Likewise books explore a compassionate, active faith lived out in real time. When we're skeptical about the status quo, Likewise books challenge us to create culture responsibly. When we're confused about who we are and what we're supposed to be doing, Likewise books help us listen for God's voice. When we're discouraged by the troubled world we've inherited, Likewise books encourage us to hold onto hope.

In this life we will face challenges that demand our response. Likewise books face those challenges with us so we can act on faith.

likewisebooks.com